Kings Cross Nut

Dry Martini (6 parts Gin and 1 part Vermouth)

# COCKTAILS AND MIXED DRINKS

PHOTOGRAPHER Reg Morrison
EDITOR Judith Dine
DESIGNER Dominique Clarke
First published by Paul Hamlyn Pty. Ltd. 1972
©Copyright Paul Hamlyn Pty. Ltd. 1972
This edition published by The Hamlyn Publishing Group Limited
1973   London • New York • Sydney • Toronto
Hamlyn House, Feltham, Middlesex, England
Printed in Hong Kong by Lee Fung
ISBN 0 600 31819 2

# COCKTAILS AND MIXED DRINKS

## Eddie Tirado

HAMLYN
London · New York · Sydney · Toronto

# ACKNOWLEDGMENTS

To all the members of the Australian Bartenders' Guild I wish to express my appreciation for the kind assistance given in the compilation of this book. To our Vice-President, James Smith and Committee Members, friends in the wine and spirit trade, I am also grateful for the help they have given.

Special thanks are due to: Mr Gordon Aldridge, The Chevron Hotel, Kosta-Boda (Aust.) Pty Ltd., Mr Bruce Boughton, Mr John Bryant, Mr Ron Hamilton, Mr Roy Mayer, Mr Alan Quayle, Mr Ray Stehr, and Mr Lou Tuttle.

Further thanks are due to my wife Judith for her patient preparation of the manuscript, and to the many people who have patronised the bars in which Australian Bartenders' Guild members work.

Eddie Tirado

# CONTENTS

# PREFACE

The Australian Bartenders' Guild has an interesting history. Originally the Australian Bartenders were affiliated with the United Kingdom Bartenders' Guild but in 1966 they broke away to form their own Guild with rules based on those of the International Bartenders' Association, of which the United Kingdom Bartenders' Guild is also an active member.

The objects of the Guild are to promote generally the interests of the trade in which the members are engaged by encouraging a higher standard of competence and conduct, to assist in the training of members, to provide for the registration of new cocktails and mixed drinks through the media of competitions and to organise other such events as lectures by the trade, and such functions as the committee may decide upon.

The Australian Guild became a member of the International Bartenders' Association in 1971, and was fortunate to send competitors to Tokyo to represent Australia for the first time in the International Cocktail Competition. The Australians returned home with fifth prize which was a wonderful effort as we competed against twenty-three other countries. Being a member of this International Guild helps to promote interest in the trade and to maintain customer service and to standardise mixed drinks.

The aim of this book is to provide a service to the barman and moreso to the home bartender. It is designed to help the host enjoy entertaining in his home and particularly to guide the young adult who is now becoming cognisant with alcoholic beverages.

Speaking as a bartender of long standing, I cannot stress strongly enough that he who drinks should do so sanely and moderately.

Eddie Tirado
President of The Australian Bartenders'
Guild

# INTRODUCTION

The origin of the cocktail is obscure but we do know that it was first made popular in America and from there, as drinking habits grew more sophisticated, its popularity has spread throughout the world.

The number of cocktail recipes available is virtually limitless and a creative barman can find endless inspiration for really original drinks at any time. This book aims to simplify cocktail mixing for the man who likes to entertain at home and to teach him the basics of mixing cocktails so that he will then want to experiment and even devise new cocktails.

# What is a Cocktail?

'Vive le cocktail' toasted a Frenchman in Betsy's Tavern near Yorktown during the American Revolution after seeing bottles decorated with cocks' tails. He was probably thinking more about the chicken he was eating than the drink but this is the American version of how the name 'cocktail' originated. Another definition of the word cocktail refers to the special way of cutting a horse's tail. However, the connection between a horse's tail and drinking a rather delicate blend of spirit, liquor and fruit juice has us baffled. But we are not concerned with the fact that we were not involved in this international farce of who invented cocktails, we just enjoy drinking them.

The word cocktail, when put in front of the word bar in any of our hotels or eateries, should cultivate thoughts of pleasant surroundings, quiet background music, sometimes even a pianist, and subdued lighting, and behind the bar stands the cocktail barman. This man, who provides not only good spirits, but a ready smile, a friendly word, a sympathetic ear and even a shoulder to cry upon, also has that little bit more knowledge about drinks and their mixing than anyone else. He takes his task of mixing your drink most seriously as he realises that he has a standard to maintain.

A cocktail is in fact a drink consisting of two or more ingredients, stirred or shaken, as a short or long drink as required. It has been said that the first cocktail was a martini but this cannot be proved, but we can take it with an olive or a twist of lemon — not a pinch of salt!

For the 'mixologist', or the host at home mixing his own concoction, there are two set rules for mixing:
1. All clear drinks, i.e. those not containing fruit juice, cream or milk, must be stirred with ice, e.g. Martinis and Manhattans.
2. Those drinks containing fruit juices and cream, etc. must be shaken either by hand or with an electric blender to acquire a perfect blend, e.g. Brandy Alexander.

# Further Tips for Successful Drink Mixing

- If possible pour your cocktails into chilled glasses for a warm cocktail is undrinkable. Chill the glasses either in the refrigerator or by putting three cubes of ice in the glass while you are mixing the drink and then discarding these ice cubes just before serving the drink. Equipment for chilling glasses is also now available in the shops.
- Almost all drinks taste better when served ice cold, therefore have plenty of clear, clean ice on hand when you entertain. The ice should be shaved, cracked or in cubes. Ice should always be placed in the mixing glass, shaker or glass before liquor is added for this chills the drink quickly and thoroughly.
- If only cubed ice is available place ice in a tea towel and hit with a mallet on hard surface to obtain cracked ice. Do **not** use glass bottle for crushing ice.
- Wherever possible use fresh lemon or orange juice in a drink. However, concentrated juice is almost as good. Keep slices of orange, lemon or lime fresh, by covering with a damp cloth and placing in the refrigerator.
- When cutting lemon, orange or lime peel, never include the white membrane of the rind. Shave off only the coloured surface peel in strips about ½ to ¾ inches wide.
- Don't fill the shaker so full that there is no room for shaking. Use a short, sharp shaking action (do not rock) when mixing cocktails.
- Cocktails should be drunk as soon as possible after serving.
- Be sure that your glasses are clean and polished and have no chips or cracks.
- Always handle glasses by the stem or base.
- Cherry or peel is always added to the cocktail after it has been shaken or mixed.
- Where a twist of orange or lemon peel is stated the oil of the peel should be squeezed on top of the cocktail and the peel is then dropped in the drink unless otherwise requested.
- Always bear in mind that bad mixing and bad presentation will ruin any cocktail or mixed drink no matter how good the recipe or the ingredients.

NOTE: All ounce measures in this book refer to the fluid ounce. American readers should note that the standard measuring cup holds 8 fluid ounces; the American pint is 16 fluid ounces whereas the Imperial pint (used in Britain and Australia) holds 20 fluid ounces.

# Setting up Your Own Bar

One of the most important assets the home entertainer can have is a bar and the necessary equipment for mixing and serving drinks. This bar can vary from the elaborate to the very simple; from a complete room set aside as a bar area in a house to a table or traymobile being used for this purpose beside a swimming pool or on the patio. If you have the time, patience and skill, you can make your own bar, if not then you can purchase a bar from any of the large department stores.

There are many types of bars but they mainly fall into three categories – mobile or portable, semi-permanent and permanent.

THE MOBILE BAR
This bar can be moved from place to place which enables you to entertain in such areas as the patio, barbecue and swimming pool at the same time, for it allows you to move, as a whole unit, your equipment, glasses and spirits, etc. to the area from which you wish to serve. The main drawback to this type of bar is the lack of washing facilities for glasses.

There are many variations of the mobile bar and a popular one is the small imitation keg which opens out showing the provision for glasses and a few bottles within.

THE SEMI-PERMANENT BAR
This type of bar tends to be a feature of the room, e.g. a cocktail cabinet, whereas a portable bar is easily hidden from view. An advantage of the semi-permanent bar is that you are able to attractively and conveniently display your equipment and glasses and even the range of spirits you have available. But keep in mind when positioning this bar that it must be as close as practicable to washing facilities.

THE PERMANENT BAR
This bar forms an integral part of the interior decoration and design of a room. It can be set up in a fashion where everything is readily accessible to the person serving drinks. In this bar, if finance is available, you can really let your head go by installing a sink with hot and cold water, refrigerator and all number of 'non-essential' bar luxuries. And on this bar your equipment and spirits can be displayed at best advantage. To be really eye-catching and effective this bar must be a showpiece in the room. Ideally the front of the bar should be illuminated by indirect lighting as should the area behind the bar. Lighting plays a most important part in the usefulness and appearance of the bar but it should be subdued. As well, the lighting, if used properly, will enhance the interior of the room in which the bar is situated.

# Shelving

Shelves of glass on the wall behind the bar look attractive. To hold the shelves use metal strips with brackets which fit at various intervals into these strips. These can be purchased in various colours from most hardware stores. This type of shelving can be adjusted for displaying glasses or bottles, and it provides an ideal place for showing off fine glassware, spirits and any other items and knick-knacks.

If you decide to build your own bar, bear in mind that the height of the bar should be comfortable for a person to sit at with his drink resting on the top of the bar. Between 3 feet and 3 feet 6 inches is best and enables you to use an ordinary kitchen stool as a bar stool. Bar stools can be expensive but a handyman with a flair for upholstery can take a piece of foam covered with vinyl and transform a kitchen stool into an attractive bar stool.

# Bar Equipment

The following basic equipment should be acquired: cocktail shaker (most popular is the 'Boston'; or 'American' or 'Standard'), or if you have a blender better still; mixing glass and spoon; spirit measures ½ and 1 ounce; ice bucket and tongs; 'Hawthorn' strainer; corkscrew; can opener; bottle opener; fruit squeezer; fruit knife and board which can double as a cheese board; swizzle sticks; toothpicks; coasters; serviettes; soda syphon; salt and pepper; nutmeg; cinnamon; a cloth for drying glasses; bottle stoppers for recorking carbonated drinks; oranges; lemons; maraschino cherries; olives and cocktail onions; straws.

# Basic Bottle Stock Required to Serve Standard Cocktails

Scotch Whisky
Bourbon Whiskey
Rye Whisky
Brandy
Cognac
Gin
Vodka
White Rum
Dark Rum
Dry and sweet vermouth
Grenadine
Angostura bitters and orange bitters

LIQUEURS
Advokaat
Cherry Brandy
Crème de Cacao
Crème de Menthe
Cointreau
Drambuie
Galliano

Grand Marnier
Tia Maria
There are many other liqueurs available so check the glossary on page
114 for taste preferences and then buy accordingly.

SOFT DRINKS AND JUICES
Soda water
Dry ginger ale
Cola
Lemonade
Bitter lemon
Tonic water
Spa water or your favourite mineral water
Orange juice
Lemon juice
Lime juice
Pineapple juice
Tomato juice

# Glasses for the Bar

Glass is a hard, brittle and usually transparent substance made by fusing
silica, an alkali, and a base. Legend ascribes its invention to the
Phoenicians and the general manufacturing process has varied little from
ancient Egypt to modern Europe. The champagne glass (as we know it
in Australia) has an interesting history. In the eighteenth century King
Louis XVI considered Marie Antoinette such a creature of beauty that
a glass should be designed to cover her breast and thus the champagne
glass was born. A further stipulation was that only the wine of France
was to be drunk from this shaped glass. This type of champagne glass
is no longer used in Europe because its width allows the gas to escape
causing the champagne to go flat in a short time. The tulip-type glass
is popularly used by champagne drinkers today, for its length helps retain
gas in champagne for a much longer period.
   A well-mixed drink will taste good no matter in what type of glass
it is served. A badly made drink will taste no better in an expensive goblet.
However, custom has established that certain drinks can be better served
in certain shapes of glasses.
   A well-equipped bar needs the following glasses:
a shot glass (used for straight spirit without ice — very common in U.S.A.
for 'Boilermakers'); 1 oz liqueur glass; 3-4 oz sherry glass; 5 oz stemmed
wine glass; 7 oz stemmed wine glass; whisky glass (sizes vary); 3 oz
cocktail glass; 6 oz champagne glass; 6 oz old-fashioned glass; 10 oz
highball glass; beer glasses (see page 66, for sizes vary); brandy balloon
or snifter.
   Whether your glassware is costly crystal or cheaper ware from the
supermarket take great care of it. Wash each glass separately in reasonably
hot water, rinse, and then dry with a clean, lint-free glass-cloth while
glass is still warm from the water. Glasses should be aired before they
are returned to their shelves. Handle glasses by the stem or base so they
retain their high polish for later use.

# What is Meant by Proof Spirit?

Proof spirit is a measure of the alcoholic content of a beverage. The term originally arose from the old custom's method of checking alcoholic content. The liquid was applied to gunpowder and if when touched with a flame, the gunpowder ignited, the liquid was termed 100 percent proof. By modern measurement, this is equivalent to 49 percent by weight of alcohol.

# Giving a Party and Enjoying It

Hospitality has two essential components: a sincere and congenial host and good preparation. Always keep your kitchen cupboard well-stocked in case of unexpected guests and make sure your bar contains a fair supply of drinks.

For a dinner or supper party choose the menu well beforehand and prepare as much of the food as possible the previous day. Of course there are always last minute jobs so allow time for these. So dress first and attend to those last minute details afterwards so that when your first guest arrives you appear to be ready.

Make sure the flowers are nicely arranged, the table set, music ready, ash trays everywhere, and bowls of savouries and snacks scattered around the room. Leave serviettes in a prominent place and provide soap, guest towels and extra toilet rolls in the bathroom.

Once you have organized your main supplies of food and refreshments take a mental check (or even have a prepared list) to make sure you have everything you are likely to need. In the bar you should have two glasses per guest, serving trays, water jugs, soda syphon, bar tools, knife and board for cutting on, fruit juice, fresh cream, oranges, lemons, cucumber, pickled onions, Maraschino cherries, mint, toothpicks, glass-cloths, sponge for mopping up, and an abundance of party ice for cooling and for mixing drinks.

Once the party is off the ground you as host must keep it from becoming boring. Introduce people and at the same time add a point of information about their job, or similar, so that there is a starting point for conversation. Delegate shy people with small jobs such as handing around savouries, collecting glasses and seeing they get back into service, for this gives them a chance to mingle. Keep the guests circulating and an old trick is to put the food at the opposite end of the room to the drink.

## GUIDE TO LIQUOR REQUIREMENTS

There is no way to calculate exactly but working on the assumption that you serve 1 oz of spirit per drink, a 26 oz bottle will produce 26 drinks. The exception to this is the aperitifs which call for 2 oz to 3 oz per drink. The average cocktail glass contains 3 oz of liquid comprised of spirit or liqueur and the basic ingredients of fruit juices or cream. Your needs will vary depending on the size of the drinks (if you value your carpet never fill the glass to the top) and the mood of your guests. It is wise to be overstocked as one very well-known toast implies:

'One bottle for the four of us! Thank God there are no more of us!'

Always allow 2 glasses per person for each type of drink served.

## BASIC DRINK STOCK

The following is a guide to basic stock required, but if you know your guests' preferences, this can be adjusted.

1.  Scotch and/or a blended whisky; Vodka; gin; rum; brandy; dry and sweet vermouth; sherry or Dubonnet; red and white wine (economically obtained in flagons) and of course beer.
2.  Soft drinks should include soda water, dry ginger, tonic water, bitter lemon, lemonade, your favourite cola, orange and lemon squash, mineral water (optional) and do not forget a bottle of bitters.
3.  Juices, either fresh or frozen should consist of tomato, orange, lemon, pineapple, lemon and lime.
4.  Garnishes to have on hand are lemons, oranges, cherries and olives.

## HELPFUL HINTS FOR THE BARMAN-HOST (See also page 8)

Carbonated beverages should be the last ingredient added to a drink.

A good tip if you are planning drinks containing sugar — make up in advance a sugar syrup containing 1 cup of sugar added to 1 cup of water. Bring to the boil and simmer until sugar is dissolved. This can be bottled and refrigerated and will keep indefinitely. It cuts down the barman's job of trying to dissolve sugar in drinks necessitating its use.

As with food or snacks, prepare the bar in advance. Fruit juices should be squeezed and oranges and lemons which are required for garnishing should be sliced fairly thick, about ¼" as they do not curl or drop. When cutting peel for a twist, take only the coloured rind, not the pulp as it is bitter. Pre-cut fruit into slices and twists and they will keep fresh if covered by a damp cloth or plastic wrap and stored in the refrigerator.

If your washing machine is handy to the kitchen, it can be a good place to store ice as it keeps cold and avoids mess of melting.

Do not forget the teetotallers at the party, and have a choice of non-alcoholic drinks for them.

So with good preparation beforehand, congenial company, well-mixed drinks and attractively presented dishes you will be a relaxed host and your party will swing.

## MEASURES

Measurements for the drink recipes have been based on Standard Imperial measures. A dash is equal to 1/6 of a teaspoon (or the equivalent to a flick of the wrist) but add the amount to suit individual tastes; 1 teaspoon = 1/6 fl. oz; 1 tablespoon = 3/5 fl. oz; 1 jigger = 1 fl. oz; 1 gill = 5 fl. oz = ¼ pint; 1 pint = 20 fl. oz = 10 to 12 servings. Unless stated otherwise the quantity in each recipe is for making one drink.

We now hope that you have gained enough knowledge and interest to set up your own bar and to purchase some of the basic equipment mentioned previously. And with the recipes for cocktails, and short and long drinks which follow for your guidance and inspiration, you should have all the necessary ingredients for a perfect barman-host.

# WHISKY BASED DRINKS

Whisky is a spirit obtained from distillation of a fermented mash (prepared ingredients before fermentation) of grain (barley, maize and rice mainly) and aged in wood.

There are approximately 200 brands of whiskies available and they vary in taste from distiller to distiller. There is no similarity of taste between Scotch, Irish, Canadian or the two American whiskies—Rye and Bourbon.

NOTE: The correct spelling is: Scotch, Canadian and Rye = Whisky.

Irish, Bourbon, Tennessee and Blended = Whiskey.

'Here's to beefsteak when you are hungry, Whisky when you are dry,
All the girls you ever want, And heaven when you die.'

# SCOTCH WHISKY

Scotch Whisky is a distinctive product of Scotland where it is believed that the first whisky was born in the Highlands in the sixteenth century. Its Gaelic name 'Usquebaugh' meaning 'water of life' was later anglicised to 'whisky'.

Two types of whiskies are necessary to produce Scotch — Scotch malt whisky which gives the blend body and character, and Scotch grain whisky which is used for lightness. In the production of Scotch two distillation processes are used: (a) the pot-still process (b) the patent (or coffey)-still process.

Scotch malt whisky is made from malted barley only and is manufactured by the pot-still process:

1.  Cleaning — the barley is cleaned to remove any foreign matter.
2.  Malting — the selected barley is steeped in water for two or three days. It is then spread on a concrete floor to germinate for eight to twelve days while the starch in the barley kernels is converted into sugar.
3.  Drying and grinding — growth is stopped at a certain time and the barley is subjected to heat over fires of smokeless coal and peat; the peat imparting its flavour and aroma during this process. The dried malt is then ground.
4.  Mashing — the ground barley is crushed with hot water and the conversion of soluble starch into maltose is completed. The liquid produced (wort) is drawn off and the remaining husks removed for cattle food.
5.  Fermentation — the wort is cooled and then passed into vessels called washbacks where it is fermented by yeast which attacks the sugar and converts it into crude alcohol, known as 'wash'
6.  Distillation — malt whisky is distilled twice in pot-stills. The 'wash' is heated, and as alcohol has a lower boiling point than water, it becomes vapour which is then cooled and condensed back into liquid.
7.  Maturation — this new whisky is poured into oak wood casks where it is matured into a pleasant mellow spirit for as long as fifteen years.

'May friendship, like whisky, improve as time advances, and may we always have old whisky, old friends, and young ones.'

Scotch on the Rocks

Irish Coffee

Scotch grain whisky is made from unmalted barley with a mixture of maize, and distilled by the patent-still process which differs from the pot-still process in four ways:

(a)   The mash consists of a proportion of malt and unmalted cereals.

(b)   The grain and water are agitated by stirrers during steam pressure cooking to burst the starch cells in the grain and to convert starch into maltose.

(c)   The liquid (worts) is collected at specific gravity lower than that produced in the pot-still process.

(d)   Distillation by this still is a continuous process and the spirit is collected at a much higher strength and does not require as long to mature as malt whisky distilled in the pot-still.

After the malt whiskies and grain whiskies are matured, they are blended or 'married' to achieve consistent quality and bouquet. There may be as many as forty different malt and grain whiskies blended according to a secret formula handed down from generation to generation, to produce the Scotch Whisky we know today.

# Blue Blazer

| | |
|---|---|
| 2 oz Scotch | lemon peel |
| 2 oz boiling water | 2 mugs |
| sugar | |

Using two silver or copper mugs:
Pour whisky into one mug and boiling water into the other.
Ignite the whisky and while burning mix both ingredients by pouring five times from one mug to the other.
Sugar to taste.
Decorate with lemon peel and serve.

# Bobby Burns

| | |
|---|---|
| ½ Scotch | 1 dash Benedictine |
| ¼ dry vermouth | ice cubes |
| ¼ sweet vermouth | lemon peel |

Stir Scotch, dry and sweet vermouth and Benedictine with ice and serve in 2½ oz cocktail glass.
Garnish with twist of lemon peel.

# Boilermaker

Serve 1 large jigger of Scotch straight with glass of beer as chaser.

# Mamie Taylor

2 oz Scotch                    ginger ale
ice                            slice of lemon

Serve Scotch in 10 oz glass with ice.
Top with ginger ale and slice of lemon.

# Morning Glory

1½ oz Scotch                   ice
white of egg                   soda water
1 teaspoon castor sugar

Shake Scotch, egg white and castor sugar, then strain into 10 oz glass
with ice.
Top with soda water and serve.

# Rob Roy

½ Scotch                       ice
½ sweet vermouth               1 Maraschino cherry
1 dash Angostura bitters

Stir Scotch, vermouth and bitters in mixing glass with ice.
Pour into 3 oz cocktail glass.
Add cherry and serve.

# Rusty Nail

1½ oz Scotch                   ice
1½ oz Drambuie                 lemon peel

Pour Scotch and Drambuie over ice in old-fashioned glass.
Serve with twist of lemon peel.

# Scotch Mist

ice
2 oz Scotch

twist of lemon peel

Three-quarter fill old-fashioned glass with ice.
Pour Scotch into shaker.
Add twist of lemon peel.
Shake and pour into old-fashioned glass unstrained on the rocks and
serve.

# Whisky Cobbler

cracked ice
2 oz Scotch
4 dashes Curaçao
4 dashes brandy

1 slice of lemon
fruit for decoration
sprig of mint

Fill goblet with cracked ice.
Add Scotch, Curaçao, brandy and slice of lemon.
Stir and decorate with fruit and sprig of mint, and serve.

# Whisky Milk Punch

2 oz Scotch
½ pint milk
1½ teaspoons sugar

ice
nutmeg

Shake Scotch, milk and sugar with ice and strain into a 10 oz glass.
Sprinkle nutmeg on top and serve.

# Whisky on the Rocks

See photograph opposite page 16.

Serve 2 oz Scotch in old-fashioned glass with ice.

# Popular Drinks

Some very popular Scotch-based drinks are:
1 oz Scotch over ice topped up with soda water.
For variation try a lemon peel in your Scotch.
Scotch with dry ginger ale.
Scotch with spa water.
Scotch with coke.

# IRISH WHISKEY

Irish Whiskey is made from a mash of cereal grains, mostly barley with perhaps 20 percent oats and wheat, in a manner similar to the malts of Scotland and it is distilled in pot-stills. (A pot-still is an old-fashioned, fat-bellied, tapered neck still requiring two distinct operations to produce a useful spirit. It is used exclusively for straight whiskies.) Triple distillation and long maturation contribute to the uniqueness of Irish Whiskey for even the youngest is aged in sherry casks for at least seven years. Irish Whiskeys were mostly straight whiskeys but now a number of blended (malt and grain) are available and are found to be a lighter-bodied product.

The Irish have many toasts to compliment their whiskey and the following is just one:

> 'Health and long life to you
> Land without rent to you
> The woman of your choice to you
> More land every year to you
> And rest in Erin.'

'May we ever be able to serve a friend and noble enough to conceal it.'

# Irish Coffee

See photograph opposite page 17.

hot black coffee
sugar

1 ½ oz Irish Whiskey
lightly-whipped fresh cream

Fill an 8 oz glass with hot black coffee.
Add sugar to taste.
Add Irish Whiskey.
Float cream on top.
Do not stir.
Serve.


# Irish Eyes

Created by Eddie Tirado

1 ½ oz Irish Whiskey
2 oz green Crème de Menthe
2 oz fresh cream

ice
1 Maraschino cherry

Shake whiskey, Crème de Menthe and fresh cream with ice and strain
into a champagne glass.
Garnish with cherry on toothpick and serve.


# Irish on the Rocks

Pour 1 ½ oz Irish Whiskey into glass of ice and serve.


# Leprechaun Dancer

Created by Eddie Tirado

2 oz Irish Whiskey
2 oz lemon juice
ice

soda water
dry ginger ale
lemon peel

Serve whiskey and lemon juice with ice in a 10 oz glass.
Top with soda water and dry ginger ale in equal parts.
Put twist of lemon peel in glass.

# CANADIAN WHISKY

The principal grains used in Canadian Whisky are corn, rye and barley malt. The proportion of grain used, and the distilling and re-distilling processes are the trade secrets of the master distiller. Canadian Whisky is a product of blended whiskies which may be blended before ageing or during the ageing period. Maturation takes place in charred white oak barrels for two or more years but most Canadian Whiskies are at least six years of age.

'Here's to good old whisky so amber and so clear.
'tis not so sweet as woman's lips but a damned sight more sincere.'

22

# Blinker Cocktail

½ oz Canadian Whisky
¾ oz grapefruit juice

¼ oz Grenadine
cracked ice

Shake whisky, grapefruit juice and Grenadine with cracked ice.
Serve in chilled cocktail glass.

# Boomerang Cocktail

1 oz Canadian Whisky
¾ oz dry vermouth
¾ oz Swedish Punch

2 dashes lemon juice
ice

Shake whisky, vermouth, Punch and lemon juice with ice.
Strain into 3 oz cocktail glass and serve.

# Carlton Cocktail

1 oz Canadian Whisky
½ oz orange juice

½ oz Cointreau
cracked ice

Shake whisky, orange juice and Cointreau with cracked ice.
Strain into chilled 2½ oz cocktail glass and serve.

# Deshler Cocktail

¾ oz Canadian Whisky
¾ oz Dubonnet
2 dashes Cointreau
2 dashes bitters

cracked ice
1 strip lemon peel
1 strip orange peel

Shake whisky, Dubonnet, Cointreau and bitters with cracked ice.
Strain into chilled 3 oz cocktail glass.
Twist lemon and orange peel over drink and serve.

# Edward VIII Cocktail

1½ oz Canadian Whisky
1 dash Pernod
2 teaspoons Italian Vermouth

2 teaspoons water
1 piece orange peel
ice

Stir whisky, Pernod, vermouth, water and orange peel with ice in old-fashioned glass and serve.


# Manhattan (Dry)

1½ oz Canadian Whisky
¾ oz dry vermouth
1 or 2 dashes Angostura bitters(optional)

ice
twist of lemon or olive

Stir whisky, vermouth and bitters with ice and strain into 3 oz cocktail glass.
Add twist of lemon or olive and serve.


# Manhattan (Sweet)

Same ingredients as previous recipe except that sweet vermouth is used instead of dry. 1 dash Angostura bitters (optional).
Garnish with a Maraschino cherry instead of lemon.


# New York Cocktail

2 oz Canadian Whisky
juice of ½ lemon
4 dashes Grenadine

ice
orange peel

Shake whisky, lemon juice and Grenadine with ice.
Strain into 3 oz cocktail glass.
Decorate with twist of orange peel and serve.

# Ward 8

1 ½ oz Canadian Whisky
1 oz lemon juice
¼ oz Grenadine

½ teaspoon powdered sugar
cracked ice
fruit for decoration

Shake whisky, lemon juice, Grenadine and sugar with cracked ice.
Strain into 3 oz cocktail glass.
Decorate with fruit.
Serve with drinking straws.

# Ward Eight
(another version)

1 ½ oz Rye Whisky
½ oz orange juice
½ oz lemon juice

1 tsp Grenadine
cracked ice

Shake whisky, orange and lemon juice, and Grenadine with cracked ice.
Strain into 3 oz cocktail glass and serve.

# Popular Drinks

Some very popular Canadian Whisky drinks are:
1 oz Canadian Whisky over ice topped with soda water.
Canadian Whisky with dry ginger ale.
Canadian Whisky with coke.
Canadian Whisky with spa water.
Canadian Whisky with lemonade.
Canadian Whisky with 3 parts lemonade and 1 part dry ginger with a
twist of lemon.

# BOURBON

The Rev. Elijah Craig is credited with production of the first Bourbon
Whiskey in 1789 in Bourbon County in the United States, but it
was only 4th May, 1964, that a resolution was passed by the U.S.
Senate and The House of Representatives, that Bourbon was
recognized as a 'distinctive product of the United States'. Most
Bourbons are straight whiskeys which means that they are obtained
from a spirit distilled from grain (not less than 51 percent corn)
and aged in new charred oak barrels for at least two years.
   Sour mash whiskey is made through a variation of the
fermentation method. The distiller uses part of a previous day's
mash, instead of fresh mash and fresh yeast as in the fermentation
of Bourbon, thus each batch is 'related' to the previous batch.

'I drink to my brother . . . and all men are my brothers.'

# Bourbon Mint Julep

2 oz Bourbon
½ teaspoon sugar
4 sprigs mint
cracked ice

dash of dark rum or brandy
mint, lemon and cherry for
decoration

Muddle Bourbon, sugar and mint.
Fill 10 oz glass with cracked ice.
Add ingredients and stir till outside of glass is frosted.
Top with dash of dark rum or brandy.
Decorate with sprig of mint, lemon and cherry.
Serve with straws.

# Bourbon on the Rocks

Pour 1½ oz Bourbon over ice in old-fashioned glass.

# Lena Cocktail
(This was the winner of the International Cocktail Competition held in Tokyo in 1971)

5/10 Old Grand-dad Bourbon
2/10 Martini Rossi Vermouth
1/10 dry vermouth

1/10 Campari
1/10 Galliano
1 Maraschino cherry

Stir Bourbon, Martini Rossi Vermouth, dry vermouth, Campari and Galliano in mixing glass.
Serve with cherry.

# Popular Drinks

Some very popular Bourbon drinks are:
1 oz Bourbon over ice topped with soda.
Bourbon with coke. See photograph opposite page 48.
Bourbon with dry ginger ale.
Bourbon with lemonade.

# TENNESSEE WHISKEY

The production of Tennessee Whiskey begins with the sour mash process similar to the method described under Bourbon, but it is definitely not Bourbon. It differs in the extra steps that take place immediately after distillation when the whiskey is seeped slowly, very slowly through vats packed with charcoal. The charcoal comes from the sugar maple tree which grows in the wooded parts of the Tennessee Highlands. It is this charcoal which contributes so much to the character of Tennessee Whiskey.

An interesting sidelight on Tennessee Whiskey is the appointment in 1971 of John Laws, well-known Australian radio and television personality, as a Tennessee Squire of the Jack Daniel Distillery in Tennessee. Jack Daniel's Tennessee Whiskey is a sour mash and in its home State in U.S.A. it is known as a 'sipping Whiskey'.

To be appointed a Tennessee Squire you must have been, for a number of years, a dedicated Jack Daniel's Black drinker, and then be recommended to the Jack Daniel Distillery for appointment as a Tennessee Squire.

John Laws is the only Tennessee Squire in Australia. The 'squiredom' entitles him to be presented with a block of land in Tennessee with the compliments of the Jack Daniel Distillery. About every three months, the company writes to Mr Laws, asking his permission to cut the grass or carry out any repairs which may be needed on his property.

The Jack Daniel Distillery holds the No 1 Distillers' Licence in America and is the distiller and bottler of what is still considered one of the top sour mash whiskeys in the world. Listed among its dedicated drinkers are Frank Sinatra, Elizabeth Taylor and Sammy Davis Jnr.

No Tennessee Squire can be a member of, or associate with, any other liquor company in the world.

'Drink, pretty creature, drink!'

# Adam and Eve Old-Fashioned
Created by Eddie Tirado

1 lump sugar
1 dash bitters
soda water

3 cubes ice
2 oz Tennessee Whiskey
½ oz Galliano

Place sugar and bitters in old-fashioned glass. Add enough soda water to cover sugar.
Muddle well.
Add ice cubes.
Pour whiskey over this.
Float ½ oz Galliano on top and serve.


# Tennessee Manhattan (Dry)

1½ oz Tennessee Whiskey
¼ oz dry vermouth
1 or 2 dashes Angostura bitters

ice
twist of lemon or olive

Stir whiskey, vermouth and bitters with ice and strain into 3 oz cocktail glass.
Add twist of lemon or olive and serve.


# Tennessee Snifter

Warm a brandy balloon by pouring warm water over it.
Dry the glass. Add 3 oz Tennessee Whiskey.
Sip and enjoy the drink.


# Tennessee Sour

juice of ½ lemon
½ teaspoon sugar
2 oz Tennessee Whiskey
ice

soda water
½ slice orange
1 Maraschino cherry

Shake lemon juice, sugar and whiskey.
Strain into 6 oz sour glass.
Top up if desired with soda water.
Decorate with orange and cherry and serve.

# BLENDED WHISKEY

These whiskeys usually contain at least twenty percent (by volume or 100 proof) straight whiskey separately, or in combination with other whiskey or neutral spirits, and bottled at not less than 80 proof. (Neutral spirits are distilled at or above 190 proof.) The straight whiskeys that go into the blended whiskeys are themselves distilled and aged, and there can be as many as seventy-five different straight whiskeys and grain and neutral spirits which go into one particular blended whiskey.

'May bad luck follow you all the days of your life and never catch you.'

# Bessie and Jessie

2 oz American Blended Whiskey ice
6 oz milk
1 oz Advokaat

Shake whiskey and milk with ice and pour into highball glass.
Float Advokaat on top and serve.


# Whiskey and Water

Pour 1½ oz whiskey over 3 cubes ice in old-fashioned glass.
Top up with water and serve.

# AUSTRALIAN WHISKY

It is nearly one hundred years since whisky was first distilled in Australia, but it was not until shortly before World War II that large modern distilleries were established in this country.

Australian distilling methods are similar to those used in the United Kingdom but the difference in Australian whisky is due to locally grown cereal grains, climatic conditions and maturation. Australian whisky is aged in oak casks for more than five years. As standards of quality control and government regulations are very strict, Australians get whisky with a unique flavour and a product equal to that of other countries.

'Let's drink to our friend and host. May his generous heart, like his good whisky, only grow mellower with the years.'

Old Fashioned Cocktail (Rye Whisky)

Eddie Tirado in Hilton Bar

# Bond 7 and James
Created by Eddie Tirado

2 oz Bond 7
1 dash sweet vermouth
spa water

orange peel
1 Maraschino cherry

Put Bond 7 in highball glass, add vermouth and top up with spa water.
Serve with garnish of orange peel and cherry.


# Hot Flashes
Created by Eddie Tirado

2 oz Four Seasons Whisky
½ oz Campari
¼ oz Bianco Vermouth

ice
lemon peel

Mix whisky, Campari and vermouth with ice in a mixing glass.
Serve with lemon peel in a cocktail glass.

# BRANDY BASED DRINKS

Brandy is a distillate or a mixture of distillates obtained solely from the fermented juice or mash of grapes. If made from any other fruit, it must clearly state on the label the fruit from which it is derived, e.g. peach brandy, cherry brandy, etc. These fruit brandies are becoming increasingly popular as they are widely used in cocktails and mixed drinks.

Brandies are aged in oak casks for a minimum of two years and the usual ageing period is from three to eight years.

Brandy is produced in many countries including Australia but Cognac is only produced in the French district of Charente, in which the city of Cognac is situated. In order to be labelled Cognac, the grapes must be grown, fermented, and distilled in this area where there are seven 'districts', listed below in order of top-quality production.

1. Grande Champagne 2. Petite Champagne 3. Borderies 4. Fins Bois 5. Bons Bois 6. Bois Ordinaire 7. Bois à Terrior.

The brandies from these regions are distilled and matured separately and then blended.

Quality markings of Cognac are:

       \* One Star
      \*\* Two Stars
    \*\*\* Three Stars
  V.O. Very old
 V.O.P. Very old pale
 V.S.O. Very superior old
V.S.O.P. Very superior old pale

Another worthy French brandy is Armagnac which comes from the region of that name in the south-west of France. Armagnac is fuller bodied and drier than Cognac.

It is best to use the younger brandies for mixed drinks. The more mature and expensive brandies are better appreciated when drunk neat, however, if your pocket is large enough you can use them for mixing.

'Here's to home where strife is shut out and love is shut in.'

# American Beauty Cocktail

½ oz brandy
½ oz dry vermouth
3 dashes white Crème
    de Menthe

½ oz Grenadine
½ oz orange juice
port wine
ice

Shake brandy, dry vermouth, Crème de Menthe, Grenadine and orange juice with ice.
Strain into 3 oz cocktail glass.
Top with port wine and serve.

# B & B

½ oz Benedictine

½ oz brandy

Add brandy to Benedictine and serve in liqueur glass.

# Between the Sheets

¾ oz brandy
¾ oz Triple Sec
¾ oz rum

juice of ½ lemon
ice

Shake brandy, Triple Sec, rum and lemon juice with ice.
Strain into 3 oz cocktail glass and serve.

# Bombay Cocktail

2 oz brandy
¼ oz sweet vermouth
¼ oz dry vermouth

3 dashes Curaçao
ice

Shake brandy, sweet and dry vermouth and Curaçao with ice.
Strain into 3 oz cocktail glass and serve.

# Bosom Caresser

⅔ brandy
⅓ orange Curacao

yolk of 1 egg
1 teaspoon Grenadine

Shake brandy, Curaçao, egg yolk and Grenadine.
Pour into 3 oz cocktail glass and serve.

# Brandy Alexander

See photograph opposite page 96.

⅓ brandy
⅓ Crème de Cacao

⅓ fresh cream
nutmeg

Shake brandy, Crème de Cacao and fresh cream with ice.
Strain into 6 oz champagne glass.
Serve with nutmeg sprinkled on top.


# Brandy Lime and Soda

1½ oz brandy
½ oz lime juice
soda water

ice
slice of lemon

Top brandy and lime juice with soda water and ice.
Serve in a tall glass and garnish with slice of lemon.


# Coffee Cocktail

1 oz brandy
1 oz Port Wine
dash Curaçao
yolk of 1 egg

1 teaspoon sugar
ice
nutmeg

Shake brandy, Port Wine, Curaçao, egg yolk and sugar with ice.
Strain into 4 oz glass.
Sprinkle nutmeg on top and serve.


# Devil Cocktail

1⅓ oz brandy

1⅓ oz green Crème de Menthe

Shake brandy and Crème de Menthe.
Strain into 3 oz cocktail glass and serve.

# Jack-in-the-Box

½ Applejack Brandy          1 dash Angostura bitters
½ pineapple juice           ice

Shake brandy, pineapple juice and bitters with ice.
Pour into 3 oz cocktail glass and serve.

# Leviathan Cocktail

½ brandy                    ¼ orange juice
¼ sweet vermouth            ice

Shake brandy, vermouth and orange juice with ice.
Pour into 3 oz cocktail glass and serve.

# Sidecar

½ brandy                    ¼ lemon juice
¼ Cointreau                 ice

Shake brandy, Cointreau and lemon juice with ice.
Strain into 3 oz cocktail glass and serve.

# Stinger

⅔ brandy                    ice
⅓ white Crème de Menthe

Mix brandy and Crème de Menthe in mixing glass with ice.
Serve in 3 oz cocktail glass.

# Popular Drinks

Some very popular brandy drinks are:
1 oz brandy over ice topped with soda water.
Brandy with dry ginger ale.
Brandy with lemonade.
Brandy with coke.
Brandy with orange juice.

# GIN
# BASED
# DRINKS

Gin was first produced in Holland in the seventeenth century as a medicinal beverage due to the presence of the Juniper Berry, one of the main flavourings necessary for the production of gin.

There are two processes for making gin — distilled and compound gins. Nearly all brands are distilled. Compound gin is a simple process that mixes neutral spirits with the Juniper Berries.

Distilled gin is obtained by original distillation of mash or by the redistillation of distilled spirits, over or with Juniper Berries and other plants. The grain formula consists of 75 percent corn, 15 percent barley malt and 10 percent other grains, and the resulting spirit has to be mixed with distilled water as it is too strong to drink. As the water differs from country to country producing gin, so does the gin. Each distiller has his own secret formula which in some cases has not altered since the first distiller made gin.

Most brands use the word 'dry' and even 'London dry' on their labels. This means that the gin lacks sweetness and any pronounced aromatic flavour or bouquet. 'London dry' originally applied to gin produced near London but is now descriptive of many gins of today. Gin does not have to be aged.

There are several kinds of gin. Although 'London dry' is the most commonly used there are others not at all alike in flavour. Tom gin is a slightly more perfumed and sweeter gin; Golden gin is a dry gin and because it is aged is gold or straw-coloured but the distiller by law cannot make any age claim; Plymouth gin is the driest of all and is produced by one distiller only; the sweetest is Sloe gin, a mixture of dry gin and sloe berries; Dutch gin which is sold under the name of 'Geneva' or 'Holland' and distilled in Holland differs from English gins in that it is heavy in body and very aromatic.

'To the sacred decree of heaven — let all men be free.'

# Abbey Cocktail

2 oz gin
1 oz orange juice
1 dash Angostura bitters

1 dash Italian Vermouth
cracked ice
1 Maraschino cherry

Shake gin, orange juice, bitters and vermouth with ice.
Strain into cocktail glass.
Serve with cherry.

# Alaska Cocktail

2 oz gin
¾ oz Yellow Chartreuse

ice
lemon peel

Stir gin and Chartreuse with ice.
Strain into 3 oz cocktail glass.
Twist lemon peel over top and serve.

# Alexander Cocktail No. 2

1½ oz gin
¾ oz Crème de Cacao
½ oz fresh cream

ice
nutmeg

Shake gin, Crème de Cacao and cream with ice.
Strain into 3 oz cocktail glass.
Sprinkle nutmeg on top and serve.

# Alfonso Cocktail

½ oz dry gin
½ oz French Vermouth
1 oz Grand Marnier

4 dashes Italian Vermouth
1 dash Angostura bitters
ice

Shake gin, French Vermouth, Grand Marnier, Italian Vermouth and bitters
with ice.
Strain into 3 oz cocktail glass and serve.

# Amsterdam Cocktail

1 oz Holland Gin
½ oz orange juice
½ oz Cointreau

4 dashes orange bitters
cracked ice

Shake gin, orange juice, Cointreau and bitters with ice.
Strain into 3 oz cocktail glass and serve.


# Apricot Cocktail

1 oz gin
½ oz Apricot Brandy
½ teaspoon Grenadine

2 drops bitters
¼ teaspoon lemon juice
cracked ice

Shake gin, Apricot Brandy, Grenadine, bitters and lemon juice with ice.
Strain into 2½ oz cocktail glass and serve.


# Blue Moon Cocktail

1 oz dry gin
½ oz Crème Yvette

½ oz lemon juice
cracked ice

Stir gin, Crème Yvette and lemon juice with ice.
Strain into 2½ oz cocktail glass and serve.


# Bronx Cocktail

1 oz dry gin
½ oz orange juice
1 dash French Vermouth

1 dash Italian Vermouth
cracked ice

Shake gin, orange juice, French and Italian Vermouth with cracked ice
Serve in 2½ oz cocktail glass.

# Clover Club Cocktail

1½ oz dry gin
4 dashes Grenadine
juice of ½ lemon

1 egg white
cracked ice

Shake gin, Grenadine, lemon juice and egg white with ice.
Serve in champagne glass.

# Coronation Cocktail

½ oz dry gin
½ oz Dubonnet

½ oz French Vermouth
cracked ice

Stir gin, Dubonnet and vermouth with ice.
Strain into cocktail glass and serve.

# Fallen Angel Cocktail

1½ oz gin
2 dashes green Crème
   de Menthe

juice of ½ lemon
cracked ice
1 dash Angostura bitters

Shake gin, Crème de Menthe, bitters, and lemon juice with ice.
Strain into 3 oz cocktail glass and serve.
NOTE: In New Zealand a Fallen Angel Cocktail consists of 2 oz Amsterdam
topped with lemonade and ginger ale served in a 10 oz glass.

# French 75

1½ oz dry gin
1 teaspoon powdered sugar
juice of ½ lemon

cracked ice
3 oz champagne
twist lemon

Combine gin, sugar and lemon juice, and shake with ice.
Strain into 12 oz highball glass containing ice.
Fill glass with champagne and add twist of lemon to serve.
NOTE:   Do not stir or champagne will lose its effervescence.

# Gibson Dry

¾ oz gin
¾ oz French Vermouth

cracked ice
pickled onion

Stir gin and vermouth with ice.
Strain into chilled cocktail glass.
Serve with onion.

# Gibson Sweet

¾ oz gin
¾ oz Italian Vermouth

pickled onion
cracked ice

Stir gin and vermouth with ice.
Strain into chilled cocktail glass.
Serve with onion.

# Gilroy Cocktail

½ oz gin
½ oz Cherry Brandy
¼ oz lemon juice

¼ oz French Vermouth
1 dash orange bitters
cracked ice

Shake gin, Cherry Brandy, lemon juice, vermouth and bitters with ice.
Strain into 2½ oz cocktail glass and serve.

# Martini (Dry)

See photograph on frontispiece.

The earliest records show the Martini recipe to consist of:
½ gin and ½ dry vermouth
1 dash orange bitters (to make it
extra dry)

1 dash Angostura bitters

It is not unusual to mix a Dry Martini 10 parts gin to 1 part vermouth.
We have also known the bartender to just wave the vermouth cork over
the gin or spray on the vermouth with an atomiser. However, we
recommend the perfect recipe for a Dry Martini as:

cube ice
2½ oz dry gin

½ oz dry vermouth
olive or a twist of lemon

Into a martini mixing glass filled with cube ice gently pour gin.
Add vermouth. Stir very gently clockwise.
Strain and serve in 3 oz cocktail glass with an olive, or a twist of lemon.

# Martini (Sweet)

2 oz gin
1 oz sweet vermouth

1 Maraschino cherry

Mix gin and vermouth as above.
Serve with cherry instead of olive.

# Napoleon Cocktail

1½ oz dry gin
1 dash Fernet Branca
1 dash Dubonnet

1 dash Curaçao
cracked ice

Stir gin, Fernet Branca, Dubonnet and Curaçao with ice.
Serve in 2½ oz cocktail glass.

# New Yorker Cocktail

½ oz gin
1½ oz French Vermouth
½ oz dry sherry

1 dash Cointreau
cracked ice

Stir gin, vermouth, sherry and Cointreau with ice.
Serve in 3 oz cocktail glass.

# Orange Blossom Cocktail

1 oz gin
2 oz orange juice

cracked ice

Shake gin and orange juice with ice.
Strain into 3 oz cocktail glass and serve.

# Perfect Cocktail

1½ oz dry gin
¾ oz dry vermouth

¾ oz sweet vermouth

Stir gin, dry and sweet vermouth.
Serve in 3 oz cocktail glass.

# Pink Gin

3 dashes Angostura bitters
2 cubes ice

1½ oz gin
1 oz water

In a goblet put 3 dashes bitters. Rotate in glass.
Throw out bitters. Add ice cubes, gin and water, and serve.

# Pink Lady No. 1

4 dashes Grenadine
4 dashes Applejack Brandy
2 oz dry gin

4 dashes fresh cream
ice

Shake Grenadine, Applejack, gin and cream with ice.
Strain into champagne glass and serve.

# Pink Lady No. 2

4 dashes Grenadine
2 oz gin

1 dash egg white

Shake Grenadine, gin and egg white.
Strain into cocktail glass and serve.

# Queen's Cocktail

1 part dry gin
1 part dry vermouth
1 part sweet vermouth

1 part pineapple juice
1 Maraschino cherry
1 piece pineapple for decoration

Shake gin, dry and sweet vermouth and pineapple juice.
Serve in cocktail glass with pineapple and cherry.

# Rolls Royce

1 oz gin
½ oz dry vermouth
½ oz sweet vermouth

¼ oz Benedictine
cracked ice

Stir gin, dry and sweet vermouth and Benedictine with ice.
Strain into 3 oz cocktail glass and serve.

# San Francisco

1½ oz Sloe Gin
¼ oz sweet vermouth
¼ oz dry vermouth
1 dash orange bitters

1 dash Angostura bitters
ice
1 Maraschino cherry

Stir gin, sweet and dry vermouth, orange and Angostura bitters with ice in mixing glass.
Add cherry.
Serve in 3 oz cocktail glass.

# Sherry Cocktail

1 oz gin
1 oz sweet sherry

1 oz lemon juice

Shake gin, sherry and lemon juice.
Strain into 3 oz cocktail glass and serve.

# Virgin Cocktail

1 oz dry gin
¾ oz white Crème de Menthe

¾ oz Forbidden Fruit
1 Maraschino cherry

Shake gin, Crème de Menthe and Forbidden Fruit.
Strain and serve with cherry in 3 oz cocktail glass.

# White Lily

1 part Cointreau
1 part Bacardi Rum

1 part dry gin
1 dash Ricard

Stir Cointreau, rum, gin and Ricard in mixing glass.
Serve in 3 oz cocktail glass.

# Popular Drinks

Some very popular gin drinks are:
1 oz gin over ice and topped with tonic water. See photograph opposite page 48.
Gin with bitter lemon.
Gin with lemonade.
Gin with coke.
Gin with lemon squash.

# RUM BASED DRINKS

'Rumbullion' meaning 'rumpus' was the drink of the slaves on plantations in the British West Indies as early as the seventeenth century, and from this came the drink we know as rum today. Rum is made basically of sugar cane by-products and is produced in most sugar-growing countries. Puerto Rico is a big rum producer, and other suppliers are British West Indies, Venezuela, Brazil, Jamaica and Australia.

It is the amount of burnt sugar cane syrup, or caramel, that gives colour and flavour to the drink and rum comes in a range of colours and flavours: there are three main types — white, gold and black label. Puerto Rican rums are blends of aged rums distilled at a high proof for lightness and dryness and aged from one to three years. White and gold labels are produced there, the gold being sweeter and darker than the white. The Jamaicans produce gold and black label, the black being richer, darker and more heavy-bodied than the gold. These are aged in oak casks.

'Here's to love, the only fire against which there is no insurance.'

# Bacardi Cocktail

3 parts Bacardi (white)
1 part lemon juice
1 dash Grenadine

1 dash egg white
1 Maraschino cherry

Shake Bacardi, lemon juice, Grenadine and egg white.
Strain into cocktail glass.
Garnish with cherry on toothpick and serve.


# Daiquiri

3 parts Bacardi (white)
1 part lemon or lime juice

3 dashes of Gomme Syrup or
1 teaspoon sugar

Thoroughly shake Bacardi, lemon or lime juice, Gomme Syrup or sugar.
Strain into chilled cocktail glass and serve.


# Frozen Daiquiri

Same recipe as Daiquiri.
Served in champagne glass with shaved ice and two short straws.
1 dash Maraschino (optional).


# Hot Buttered Rum

1½ oz of Jamaican Rum
1 lump sugar
small slice butter

boiling water
nutmeg

Use old-fashioned glass or mug.
Combine rum, sugar and butter.
Fill glass with boiling water over silver spoon (to prevent glass breaking) and stir.
Sprinkle nutmeg on top and serve.

# Mai Tai

2 oz light rum
1 oz Jamaican Rum
1 teaspoon sugar
½ oz lemon or lime juice
½ oz Almond Liqueur

crushed ice
sprig of mint
pineapple spear
1 Maraschino cherry

Pour light and Jamaican Rum, sugar, lemon or lime juice and Almond Liqueur into double old-fashioned glass half filled with ice.
Mix well.
Add crushed ice to fill and stir gently to combine ice with other ingredients.
Garnish with sprig of mint, a pineapple spear and a Maraschino cherry.
If Mai Tai mix is available just add spirit.

# Planter's Punch

2 oz Jamaican Rum
1 oz lemon or lime juice
1 dash Angostura bitters
1 teaspoon Grenadine

ice
soda water
lemon, orange slices
1 Maraschino cherry

Place rum, lemon or lime juice, bitters and Grenadine in 10 oz glass with ice.
Top with soda water and serve with straws.
Garnish with slice of lemon or orange and cherry.

Bourbon and Coke; Gin and Tonic; Short Gin Sling

Grasshopper

# Zombie

2 oz light rum
1 oz Jamaican Rum
½ oz Apricot Brandy
½ teaspoon powdered sugar
½ oz lemon juice
mint, pineapple, cherry for
decoration
½ oz 150 proof Demarara Rum
(if available)

1 bar-spoon (or 1 teaspoon)
Papaya nectar and/or 1
bar-spoon pineapple juice
and/or
1 bar-spoon passionfruit juice
and/or 1 bar-spoon plum or
apricot juice
shaved ice
cracked ice

Fill 14 oz zombie glass with shaved ice.
In cocktail shaker put all above ingredients, except Demarara Rum and shake well with cracked ice.
Pour unstrained into 14 oz zombie glass which is half-full of cracked ice.
Decorate with sprig of mint or pineapple spear and cherry.
Top with Demarara Rum, being careful to pour so that it floats on surface of drink.
Serve with drinking straws.

This preceding recipe is the original zombie. Below is a simple version of the zombie:

cracked ice
1 oz lemon or lime juice
4 dashes passionola or Papaya
juice
4 dashes Apricot Brandy
4 dashes Cherry Brandy
1 oz rum (white)

1 oz rum (dark)
1 oz Jamaican Rum
151 proof rum
green and red cherries for
decoration
slice of orange

Fill 14 oz zombie glass with cracked ice.
Add the above ingredients, except 151 proof rum, and stir.
Top with 151 proof rum.
Decorate with green and red cherries and slice of orange.
Serve with drinking straws.

# VODKA BASED DRINKS

Vodka was produced in Poland in the twelfth century and has been a favourite drink in Russia and Poland ever since.

It is an alcoholic distillate from a fermented mash of grain. In the making of genuine Vokda nothing is added to the neutral spirits, all character is removed leaving it odourless, tasteless, colourless and smooth, and this gives you the advantage of being able to add your favourite non-alcoholic beverage to it, thus it has become very popular in making mixed drinks. In Europe, however, Vodka is flavoured and is drunk chilled and neat. It does not need to be aged.

Because one is not aware of a flavour many people, on first experiencing Vodka-mixed drinks, can drink too much with 'disastrous' results.

'May your soul be in Glory three weeks before the Devil knows you're dead.'

# Black Russian

3 parts Vodka                    ice
1 part Kahlua

Serve Vodka and Kahlua on the rocks.
This can also be served with equal parts of Vodka and Kahlua.


# Bloody Mary

1 dash Worcestershire sauce       2oz Vodka (White Rum, gin or
2 drops Tabasco sauce             Tequila can be substituted
¼ oz lemon juice                  for Vodka)
salt and pepper                   tomato juice
3 cubes ice

In 10 oz glass put Worcestershire sauce, Tabasco sauce and lemon juice.
Add salt and pepper.
Mix together and then add ice cubes, Vodka (or substitute).
Top with tomato juice.
Serve with swizzle stick.
NOTE: For a different taste celery salt can be substituted for ordinary
salt.


# Harvey Walbanger
(Very popular)

1 oz Vodka                        orange slice and cherry for
1 oz Galliano                     garnish
orange juice

In 10 oz glass put Vodka and Galliano.
Top with orange juice.
Garnish with slice of orange and cherry and serve.


# Moscow Mule

3 cubes ice                       ginger beer
2 oz Vodka                        mint for decoration
1 oz lemon juice

In 10 oz glass put 3 cubes ice, add Vodka and lemon juice.
Fill with ginger beer.
Decorate with mint and serve.

# Russian Cocktail

1 oz Vodka                          1 oz Crème de Cacao
1 oz dry gin

Shake Vodka, gin and Crème de Cacao.
Strain into cocktail glass and serve.


# Salty Dog

3 cubes ice                         grapefruit juice
1½ oz Vodka

In 10 oz highball glass place 3 cubes ice and 1½ oz Vodka.
Top up with grapefruit juice and serve.


# Screwdriver

3 cubes ice                         slice of orange
1½ oz Vodka                         1 Maraschino
orange juice                          cherry

In 10 oz highball glass place 3 cubes ice and 1½ oz Vodka.
Top up with orange juice.
Garnish with slice of orange and cherry and serve.


# Vodka Martini

Same as Gin Martini substituting Vodka for gin.

# Vodka Mist

1½ oz Vodka                              twist of lemon

In a cocktail shaker pour 1½ oz Vodka.
Add twist of lemon.
Serve unstrained in old-fashioned glass.


# Vodka on the Rocks

3 cubes ice                              1½ oz Vodka

Pour 1½ oz Vodka over 3 cubes of ice in old-fashioned glass and serve.


# Popular Drinks

Some very popular Vodka drinks are:
1 oz Vodka over ice topped up with your favourite juice.
Vodka with coke.
Vodka with tonic.
Vodka with lemonade.
Vodka with ginger ale.

# TEQUILA

Tequila dates back to Aztec times long before the Spanish conquered the country. True Tequila must come from the city of Tequila in south-west Mexico, but most Tequilas are imported to Australia via the United States. Tequila is made from the sap of the wild Mescal plant (similar to cactus) and it is produced near the city of Tequila where the Mescal plants are abundant. The mescal is then fermented and distilled and becomes Tequila. There are two varieties — white and gold label. The white label is not aged whereas the gold is aged in used whisky barrels just long enough to impart the gold colour ready for bottling.

Tequila is reputed to have a very strong alcoholic content but it is much the same as gin or Vodka. It probably earned its mule-kick reputation because of the way the peons drank it. A piece of lemon and some salt were put on the clenched fist of the left hand. Tequila was drunk from the right hand followed by a lick of lemon and salt. Today the Mexicans drink Tequila with their own hot version of tomato juice and call it Sangrita.

'Friendship is the wine of life. Let's drink of it and to it.'

# Margarita

Tequila has achieved success as a result of the popularity of this classic cocktail. The name, Margarita, has been traced back to a famous Mexican dancer, whose dark flashing eyes and tapping heels stimulate the excitement of this drink:

salt
1½ oz Tequila
½ oz Triple Sec or Cointreau

1 oz of fresh lemon or lime juice
slice of lemon

Rim the glass with salt by first moistening the rim with slice of lemon then sprinkle salt over the moistened area.
Vigorously shake Tequila, Triple Sec or Cointreau, and lemon or lime juice.
Strain into cocktail glass.
Garnish with slice of lemon and serve.

# Tequila Cocktail

juice of ½ lemon
4 dashes Grenadine
2 oz Tequila

1 dash egg white
ice
twist of lemon

Vigorously shake lemon juice, Grenadine, Tequila and egg white with ice.
Strain into cocktail glass.
Serve with twist of lemon for garnish.

# Tequila Sour

See Sours.

# Tequila Straight

1½ oz Tequila in shot glass
1 slice of lemon

salt

Hold glass in right hand, lemon in left hand, salt on side of hand near thumb — lick salt, drink Tequila then bite into the lemon, and say 'ole' and wait for the bulls to come!

# SAKE

This rice wine is the traditional Japanese drink and is usually served warm in small cups called Sakazuki and poured from a narrow-mouthed bottle called tokkuri. Its colour can vary from clear to pale amber with each brand having a distinctive character and taste. It does not need ageing.

'Friendly may we part and quickly meet again.'

# Sake Highball

3 oz Sake
juice of ¼ lemon
1 teaspoon castor sugar

ice
soda water
slice of lemon

Stir Sake, lemon juice and castor sugar with ice and top with soda water.
Garnish with slice of lemon and serve.


# Tamagozake Cocktail

6 oz Sake
1 egg

1 teaspoon sugar

Bring sake to boil and light with match.
Allow to burn for 1 second.
Remove from heat.
Add egg and sugar and stir.
Pour into drinking cup and serve.

# APERITIFS

An aperitif is a drink taken to stimulate one's appetite and is usually a wine based cocktail.

'May the Devil cut the toes off our foes that we may know them by their limping.'

# Black Power

2 oz Marsala (dessert wine)    3 cubes ice
coca-cola    slice lemon

Top Marsala with coca-cola over ice cubes in old-fashioned glass.
Add slice of lemon and serve.


# French Greenery

1 part Pernod    3 cubes ice
1 part Green Crème de Menthe    sprig of mint

Serve Pernod and Crème de Menthe over ice cubes in old-fashioned glass.
Add mint for decoration and serve.


The most popular four aperitifs are sherry, vermouth, Dubonnet
and Byrrh.

SHERRY was first produced in Spain near the town of Jerez.
Sherries are wines varying in colour from white to dark brown.
The four types are extra dry, dry, medium dry and sweet. Most
Spanish sherries, except the very dry ones, are distinguished by a
delightful 'nutty' taste. Sherry is served in a 2 oz sherry glass. Very
dry should be chilled, medium sherries should be slightly chilled
and sweet should be opened and left standing at room
temperature.

# Maria

2 oz sweet sherry    3 cubes ice
1 oz Beefeater's Gin    1 Maraschino cherry

Stir sherry and gin with ice cubes in mixing glass.
Strain into cocktail glass.
Serve with cherry for decoration.

VERMOUTH is probably the most popular of the aperitifs. It is made using white wine such as Muscatel, Sauterne, white port or even mild sherry as a base, and added to this are strongly flavoured wines which contain as many as fifty different herbs and spices. One of these herbs is 'Wermuth' which, in German, means wormwood. There are four types of vermouth:
Dry — sometimes known as French which is clear and dry.
Sweet — sometimes known as Italian which is red and sweet.
Bianco — which is gold in colour and is the sweetest. See photograph opposite page 64.
Amaro — which is brown in colour and is very bitter.

# Manhattan Cocktail

¾ oz sweet vermouth
1½ oz Bourbon or Canadian
Whisky
1 dash Angostura bitters
(optional)

ice
1 Maraschino cherry

Stir vermouth, whisky and bitters with ice.
Strain into cocktail glass.
Garnish with cherry and serve.

DUBONNET is a blend of carefully selected old liqueur wines to which Peruvian bark or quinine is added. It has a rich, slightly sweet flavour with the qualities of a mild liqueur. It can be served in a sherry or cocktail glass chilled, with a slice of lemon, or it can be served as a cocktail as follows:

# Dubonnet Cocktail

½ Dubonnet
½ gin

twist of lemon

Stir Dubonnet and gin with ice.
Strain into cocktail glass.
Garnish with twist of lemon and serve.

BYRRH (pronounced to rhyme with 'her') is a French wine, fortified with brandy, and with a quinine flavour. The juice of sweet and dry grapes is mixed and passed over a series of aromatic herbs and Peruvian bark to produce its stimulating taste and aroma. Serve it as follows:

# Byrrh Frappé

2 oz Byrrh                                    twist of lemon
cracked ice

Pour Byrrh into cocktail glass filled with cracked ice.
Serve with twist of lemon.

# Byrrh Freeze

2 oz Byrrh                                    slice lemon
½ oz lemon cordial                            1 Maraschino cherry
soda water                                    ice

Pour Byrrh and cordial into glass.
Top with soda water and garnish with slice of lemon and cherry.
Serve in a highball glass with ice.

NOTE:    All aperitifs are more enjoyable if complimented with a selection of cheeses and savoury biscuits.

# BEER

'Here's to sweethearts and wives, may they never meet.'

# History

The origin of brewing dates back to the time of the Pharoahs towards the end of the Fourth Dynasty. Ancient beer, known as Heqa (Rosetta Stone) came from Kati, a country to the east of Egypt.

By the year 2000 BC brewing was firmly established in Egypt. It was the daily drink for the Egyptians and was brewed from the waters of the Nile near the town of Thebes. Beer was believed to be a gift from the gods and the art of brewing was assigned to Isis, the wife of Osiris (Rameses II). Rameses promoted beer for consumption on all religious, social and state occasions.

The Greeks learned about brewing from the Egyptians and called it 'zythos' and even Sophocles recommended as the ideal diet, bread, meat, vegetables and beer.

The Romans learned the art of brewing from the Greeks.

Even in India ancient Sanskrit law refers to alcoholic beverages prepared from barley, molasses and rice, so it is not surprising that literature of the Germanic races contained references to the manufacture of beer.

Brewing in England first appeared in Roman times but during the Anglo-Saxon period brewing became firmly established. It is believed that Edward the Confessor consumed ale at a banquet prior to the Battle of Hastings in 1066.

The monastic system flourished during the Middle Ages with each monastery having its own brewery with a monk in charge of brewing, and each day he was allowed to consume two gallons of ale for tasting purposes.

Brewers often used many flavouring agents such as wormwood, alum, gentian and ground ivy and sometimes powdered oyster shells, aloes, bitter apples and bark of the pine, oak and willow. The ground oyster shells were a clarifying agent, liquorice was used for colouring and was esteemed as gently laxative; it was also believed to prevent corpulence.

Even as late as the eighteenth century leading men of science believed that fermentation was caused by an electrical influence, and even until one hundred years ago, some people believed it to be supernatural.

In 1860 when Louis Pasteur proved fermentation was caused by micro-organisms he was ridiculed by all. But later Pasteur and others confirmed the connection between yeast and the transformation of sugars by fermentation.

In Babylonian times if a glass of beer was served without a creamy head, the penalty for the barmaid was drowning, most people would agree this was severe but it shows how revered beer was in those days.

Quality control is a major part of brewing and its aim is to ensure the consistency and uniformity of the product. Each brewery has a laboratory and its task is to test and measure throughout the brewing process. Because of this beer has never been purer than it is at present.

Champagne (tulip glass); Beer; Bianco Vermouth
(Food by courtesy of Virginia de Winter of the Gallery Wine Bar)

Home cocktail bar

# Raw Materials used in Beer

BARLEY is preferred to other cereals as it can be more easily malted for brewing and the solubles extracted from barley malt are more complete than those of other grains.

When the grain has been steeped and dried, it is termed malt, and is ready for grinding or storing.

HOPS belong to the nettle family. The female plants bear cone-shaped formations which are used and which impart a bitter flavour and pleasant aroma, increasing the refreshing quality, and stimulating digestion.

Actually any cereal containing starch or sugar may be used in the brewing of beer e.g. maize, rice, corn or wheat but these grains are lacking essential enzymes (chemicals which facilitate the extraction of sugars) and when used require special treatment. If used alone the final product would not be beer as we know it in Australia.

SUGAR is an important addition as it helps to produce a beer of paler colour, less filling and a better taste and, of course, increased stability.

BREWER'S YEAST is a micro-organism belonging to the saccharomyces species and is capable of a fantastic rate of reproduction. Its work is to propagate, which it does asexually and split up the sugar component into equal quantities of alcohol and carbon dioxide ($CO_2$). At this stage it may be well to mention that it is the $CO_2$ content of beer which determines the amount of foam formation. A consistent $CO_2$ level means that the barman will not have any trouble handling beer at normal temperatures.

THE BREWING PROCESS

The barley is steeped until it germinates and then kiln-dried to 180° to stop germination, it is then termed malt and is ready for grinding. The next step is:

MASHING

The crushed malt is mixed with water at a given temperature for the proper length of time. The resultant solution 'wort' is then used to make beer and the residue (spent grain) is sold as stock fodder.

FERMENTATION

Fermentation is the next process where the yeast splits the sugars into alcohol and carbon dioxide. This is the most decisive phase in the brewing process for the attainment of brews of fine taste and aroma.

## WHAT IS LAGER BEER?

Lager beer is distinguished by the fact that the wort is fermented by yeast of a bottom fermentation type (i.e. yeast which settles to the bottom of the fermenting tanks) and then is stored in refrigerated cellars for maturing and clarification. Lager got its name from the process the German brewers used to mature their **bier** in oak vats viz. 'lagering' which means 'to store'.

## WHAT IS ALE?

Traditionally, an ale is fermented by yeast of the top fermentation type and has a more pronounced hop flavour. Nowadays this term is often applied to some bottom fermentation beers with a pronounced hop flavour.

## WHAT IS PORTER?

A top fermentation beer, porter is heavier and darker than ale, more malty in flavour, with less flavour of hops but sweeter in taste.

## WHAT IS STOUT?

Top fermented stout is similar to porter. It has a strong flavour and a sweet taste, but is heavier and has a stronger hop character than porter.

## WHAT IS PILSENER?

Pilsener is a lager beer originally from the town of Pilsen in Germany.

## GLASSES

Glasses used for beer-drinking should always be cool, clean and perfectly dry. When the beer is poured into a dry glass the air is trapped against the side and bottom of the glass and combines with the carbonic acid gas. A wet glass causes little air to be trapped and the result is flat beer.

The froth of various coloured liquids is always white. When liquids such as ales, champagnes and wines differ in colour, their froths, which are a collection of little spheres, are always white, due to the light which falls upon these and is reflected off the spheres.

# Beer Drinks

Most people like their beer as beer but there are some variations for drinks using beer. See photograph opposite page 64.
Red Eye — which is beer and tomato juice.
Boilermaker — 1 large jigger of Scotch Whisky served straight with a glass of beer as a chaser.
Shandy — beer and lemonade.

# PRIZE–WINNING COCKTAILS

'May you live every day of your life.'

# Blow Up

Created by Alex Weissenfels

cracked ice
1 oz Bacardi
1 oz Yellow Chartreuse

½ oz Bols Parfait Amour
5 drops Grenadine
5 drops Crème de Menthe

Half fill mixing glass with cracked ice.
Add Bacardi, Chartreuse and Bols Parfait Amour.
Stir and strain into 5 oz champagne glass.
Add 5 drops Grenadine and 5 drops Crème de Menthe and serve.


# Blue Haze

Created by Nick Zongas

1 oz Bacardi
½ oz Martini and Rossi Dry
Vermouth
½ oz Parfait Amour

½ oz Cointreau
Bols Blue Curaçao

Stir all ingredients except Curaçao and strain.
Add 4 dashes Curaçao after pouring and serve.


# Blue Negligee

Created by Frank Clark

⅓ Mataxa Oyzo
⅓ Marie Brizard Parfait Amour
⅓ Green Chartreuse

ice
1 Maraschino cherry

Shake all the above ingredients with ice.
Pour into cocktail glass with cherry.
Serve.

# Chocolate Peppermint
Created by Eddie Tirado

½ Black and White
Scotch Whisky

Chocolate Peppermint
liqueur

Shake Scotch and the liqueur.
Strain into cocktail glass and serve.


# Dizzy Blonde
Created by Peter Zorbas

cracked ice
2 oz Bols Advokaat
1 oz Pernod

lemonade
1 Maraschino cherry

Half fill 10 oz highball glass with cracked ice.
Add Advokaat and Pernod.
Top with lemonade.
Place slit cherry on lip of glass and serve.


# 10 Furlongs
Created by Bill Schober

1 oz Vodka
1 oz Apricot Brandy
½ oz Bols White Curaçao
3 dashes green lime

bitter lemon
½ slice pineapple
1 Maraschino cherry

Stir Vodka, Brandy, Curaçao and lime well.
Pour without straining into a 10 oz glass.
Top up with bitter lemon.
Garnish with pineapple and cherry and serve.

# Gaslight
Created by Joan Gandy

1 oz Metaxa Brandy
½ oz Apricot Brandy

1 dash Galliano

Shake all above ingredients.
Strain and serve.


# Gin Tropical
Created by Joan Gandy

1 oz Gordon's Gin
1 oz passionfruit syrup
½ oz Bols Blue Curacao

soda water
1 Maraschino cherry
slice orange

Shake gin, passionfruit syrup and Curacao.
Strain into glass and top with soda water.
Serve with drinking straws, cherry and slice of orange for garnish.


# Hawaiian Honeymoon
Created by Eddie Tirado

1½ oz Bacardi
2 oz orange juice
1 oz pineapple juice
1 dash lemon juice

1 dash Grenadine
cherry, pineapple and orange for garnish
Pernod 45

Mix Bacardi, orange juice, pineapple juice, lemon juice and Grenadine.
Float Pernod 45 on top.
Garnish with cherry, slice of pineapple and orange, and serve.

# Nickel Fever
Created by James Zorbas

⅓ oz Southern Comfort
⅓ oz Galliano
⅔ oz fresh orange juice

⅔ oz fresh cream
¼ oz Bols Blue Curacao
ice chips

Half fill cocktail shaker with ice.
Shake Southern Comfort, Galliano, orange juice, fresh cream and Curacao.
Strain into 5 oz champagne glass.
Add couple ice chips and 8 drops Blue Curaçao and serve.


# Pablo
Created by Joan Gandy

cracked ice
1 oz Bacardi
½ oz Cointreau

½ oz Bols Advokaat
1 slice pineapple
1 Maraschino cherry

Half fill cocktail shaker with ice.
Add Bacardi, Cointreau, Advokaat and pineapple.
Shake and strain into 5 oz champagne glass.
Garnish with cherry and serve.


# Paula Stafford
Created by Ian Orton

1/5 gin
2/5 Pimms No 1

2/5 Cleopatra

Shake gin, Pimms and Cleopatra.
Strain and serve.

# Peppermint Fizz
Created by Ron Clancy

2 oz peppermint chocolate
1 oz fresh cream
ginger beer

Crème de Menthe
1 Maraschino cherry

Pour chocolate with cream.
Top with ginger beer.
Float Bols Crème de Menthe.
Decorate with cherry, sprinkle chocolate on top and serve.


# Pink Elephant
Created by Peter Zorbas

cracked ice
¾ oz Vodka
¾ oz Galliano
¾ oz Crème de Noyeau or
Almond Liqueur

¾ oz fresh orange juice
¾ oz fresh cream
dash Grenadine
cinnamon for decoration

Half fill cocktail shaker with ice.
Shake all ingredients.
Strain into 5 oz champagne glass.
Sprinkle cinnamon on top and serve.


# Royal Snowcap
Created by Bill Schober

¾ oz Bacardi
¾ oz Martini and Rossi Dry
Vermouth
½ oz Bols Parfait Amour

dash lemon juice
egg white
chocolate flakes for decoration

Shake all ingredients.
Add dash lemon juice and egg white.
Decorate with chocolate flakes and serve.

# See-through
Created by Bill Schober

cracked ice
1 oz Bacardi White Rum
½ oz Cointreau

½ oz Orange Gin
1 dash Bols Blue Curacao
cocktail onion

Half fill mixing glass with cracked ice.
Gently stir Bacardi, Cointreau, gin and Curacao.
Strain into cocktail glass.
Serve with onion for garnish.


# Serpent's Sting
Created by Peter Zorbas

cracked ice
¾ oz Bacardi
¾ oz Galliano
¾ oz Crème de Noyeau or
Almond Liqueur

¾ oz fresh orange juice
¾ oz fresh cream
1 Maraschino cherry

Half fill cocktail shaker with ice.
Shake all ingredients.
Strain into 5 oz champagne glass.
Place slit cherry on lip of glass and serve.


# Smugglers' Gold
Created by Ian Orton

2 parts Scotch
1 part Forester Liqueur
1 dash lemon juice

1 dash Goldwasser Liqueur
ice

Shake Scotch, liqueurs and lemon juice with ice.
Strain into cocktail glass and serve.

# Three Orbit
Created by Eddie Tirado

1 part Drambuie
1 part Cointreau

1 part Vodka

Shake Drambuie, Cointreau and Vodka.
Strain and serve.


# Topping
Created by John Berry

¾ oz Sloe Gin
¾ oz dry vermouth
½ oz Crème de Violette

ice
1 Maraschino cherry

Place gin, vermouth, Crème de Violette with ice in cocktail shaker.
Shake and strain.
Pour into 2½ oz glass.
Add cherry and serve.


# Twilight Zone
Created by Arthur Doll

cracked ice
2 oz Bacardi
1 oz Bols Crème de Menthe
½ oz Bols Parfait Amour

½ oz lime cordial
½ oz fresh cream
1 Maraschino cherry

Half fill cocktail shaker with cracked ice.
Shake Bacardi, Crème de Menthe, Parfait Amour, cordial and fresh cream.
Strain into 5 oz champagne glass.
Garnish with cherry and serve.

# DRINK
# RECIPES

'May we have in our arms those we love in our hearts.'

# Angelique
Created by George Anamourlis

1 oz Ouzo
1 oz Advokaat
1 oz Strega

1 oz fresh cream
1 oz orange juice
1 Maraschino cherry

Shake Ouzo, Advokaat, Strega, cream and orange juice.
Pour into champagne glass.
Garnish with cherry and serve.


# Autumn Leaf
Created by Bill Schober

⅓ Arrak
⅓ Crème de Cacao

⅓ Danziger Goldwasser

Stir Arrak, Crème de Cacao and Danziger Goldwasser.
Strain into cocktail glass and serve.


# Bali Hi
Created by John Berry

¼ oz Orange Curaçao
¼ oz Mandarin Liqueur
1 oz Advokaat

Fanta
slice orange or
1 Maraschino cherry

Serve Curaçao, liqueur and Advokaat in 8 oz highball glass.
Top with Fanta and stir.
Garnish with slice of orange or cherry and serve.


# Blue Horn
Created by Jerry Kucera

½ oz Pernod 45
½ oz Blue Curaçao
1 oz Bacardi

dash of lemon juice
bitter lemon

Put Pernod, Curaçao, Bacardi and lemon juice in glass.
Top up with bitter lemon and serve in 10 oz highball glass.

# Breathaliser Buster
Created by Jerry Kucera

⅓ Crème de Menthe      ⅓ Vodka
⅓ Cointreau

Serve above ingredients in 3 oz cocktail glass.


# Chevron's Moon Landing
Created by Eddie Tirado
See photograph opposite page 80.

1 pineapple
3 cubes ice
1 oz Vodka
1 oz dark Bacardi
½ oz Apricot Brandy

½ oz Cherry Brandy
1 dash Angostura bitters
12 Maraschino cherries
lemon slices
1 olive

Slice top off pineapple about 2" from top.
Hollow out the pineapple and cut half the fruit into small squares.
Place fruit back in pineapple.
In cocktail shaker put ice cubes, Vodka, Bacardi, Apricot Brandy, Cherry Brandy and bitters, and shake.
Pour unstrained over the fruit in the pineapple shell.
Place 4 toothpicks around edge of pineapple shell and cover with 3 cherries on each toothpick.
Place 4 toothpicks in lid of pineapple to correspond with position of bottom toothpicks.
Place lid back so that toothpicks go into the cherries.
Decorate with 2 round slices of lemon ¼" thick; one slice of lemon goes on either side of pineapple.
Balance two crossed swizzle sticks on toothpick that goes through the lemon.
Secure the sticks by placing an olive on the exposed part of the toothpick.
Serve with spoon and drinking straws.


# Constellation
Created by Mac McGreggor

⅓ dark rum
⅓ Italian Vermouth
⅓ ginger wine

dash of lime juice
dash Angostura bitters

Shake rum, vermouth, ginger wine, lime juice and bitters.
Strain and serve.

# Dunk Cocktail
Created by Peter Zorbas

⅓ oz Galliano
1 oz dry gin
1/6 oz Blue Curaçao

⅔ oz dry vermouth
1 Maraschino cherry

Stir Galliano, gin, Curaçao and vermouth.
Strain into chilled cocktail glass.
Add cherry and serve.


# Editor's Curse
Created by Tony Camilleri

⅓ Scotch
⅓ Van der Hum

⅓ orange juice

Shake Scotch, Van der Hum and orange juice.
Strain into 2 oz cocktail glass and serve.


# Elephant Walk
Created by Tom Sharman

cracked ice
1 oz dry gin
½ oz Tequila
½ oz fresh orange juice
dash Grenadine

dash Angostura bitters
½ slice orange
½ slice lemon
2" stick cucumber

Fill 6 oz old-fashioned glass with cracked ice.
Add gin, Tequila, orange juice, Grenadine, and bitters.
Garnish with orange, lemon and cucumber.
Add swizzle stick and serve.


# Head Shrinker
Created by Jerry Kucera

⅓ Bacardi
⅓ Galliano

⅓ Blue Curaçao
dash Bianco Vermouth

Serve above ingredients in 3 oz cocktail glass.

# Kings Cross Nut

Created by Eddie Tirado

See photograph on frontispiece.

| | |
|---|---|
| 1 coconut | 1 oz Tia Maria |
| 3 cubes ice | nutmeg |
| 2 oz brandy | |

Take top off coconut and remove milk.
Place half the milk and ice cubes into cocktail shaker.
Add brandy, Tia Maria.
Shake and strain back into the coconut.
Dust with nutmeg.
Serve with spoon and drinking straws.


# King's Daiquiri

Created by Eddie Tirado

| | |
|---|---|
| ½ oz lemon juice | ¼ teaspoon sugar |
| ½ oz Parfait Amour | dash egg white |
| 1½ oz Bacardi | |

Blend lemon juice, Parfait Amour, Bacardi, sugar and egg white.
Serve in champagne glass.


# Machine-Gun Kelly

Created by Eddie Tirado

| | |
|---|---|
| 1½ oz Ned Kelly Whisky | dash of orange bitters |
| 1 oz sweet vermouth | twist of lemon |
| 1 oz dry vermouth | |

Shake whisky, sweet and dry vermouth and bitters.
Strain into champagne glass.
Garnish with twist of lemon and serve.


# Macleay Street

Created by James Smith

| | |
|---|---|
| 1 oz Jim Beam Bourbon | dash Grenadine |
| ½ oz Galliano | orange juice |

Top Bourbon, Galliano and Grenadine with orange juice and shake together.
Serve in 10 oz highball glass.

Chevron's Moon Landing

TOP:       Back l to r:  Martini mixing glass; American-type cocktail shaker;
                  (the glass part can double as a mixing glass); Boston cocktail
                  shaker; standard cocktail shaker.
                  Front l to r:  Angostura Bitters and Orange Bitters with sprinklers

BOTTOM: l to r clockwise:  swizzle sticks; funnel; glass ice bucket;
                  cigarette lighter; salt and pepper shakers; straws; paper serviettes;
                  coasters; fruit knife; corkscrew opener; ice tongs; bar spoon;
                  combination can opener, knife and corkscrew and bottle opener;
                  Hawthorn strainer; strainer which can double as ice scoop.
                  Centre l to r:  2 oz measure; 1 oz measure; ½ oz measure; toothpicks

# Miss Aileen
Created by James Smith

⅓ Gilbey's Advokaat          ⅓ Galliano
⅓ Royal Chocolate Mint Liqueur

Shake Advokaat, liqueur and Galliano.
Strain into 3 oz cocktail glass and serve.


# Moomba Cocktail
Created by Bill Schober

¾ oz Bacardi                    1 dash Grenadine
¾ oz Grand Marnier              ice
½ oz orange juice               orange peel
¼ oz lemon juice

Shake Bacardi, Grand Marnier, orange and lemon juice, and Grenadine
with ice.
Strain into cocktail glass.
Garnish with orange peel and serve.


# Moon Crater
Created by Eddie Tirado

1 oz Vodka                      nutmeg
1 oz Advokaat                   ice
Fanta                           1 Maraschino cherry
fresh cream

Put Vodka and Advokaat in highball glass.
Fill with Fanta and top with cream.
Dust with nutmeg.
Serve with ice in highball glass and garnish with cherry.

# Moon's Eclipse
Created by George Anamourlis

1 oz Campari
1 oz Drambuie
1 oz Amsterdam
1 oz pure orange juice

1 oz fresh cream
nutmeg
1 Maraschino cherry

Shake Campari, Drambuie, Amsterdam, orange juice and cream.
Pour into champagne glass.
Sprinkle nutmeg on top.
Garnish with cherry and serve.


# Old San Francisco
Created by Joe Zernicke

⅓ oz Kirsch
⅓ oz Keuck
2 dashes lime cordial

2 dashes Grenadine
fresh cream
Nescafe coffee

Mix Kirsch, Keuck, cordial and Grenadine.
Strain.
Float beaten cream and Nescafe on top and serve.


# Paris By Night
Created by George Anamourlis

1 oz Pernod
1 oz Strega
½ oz Amsterdam

lemonade
slice orange
1 Maraschino cherry

Put Pernod, Strega and Amsterdam, in highball glass.
Top with lemonade.
Serve in 10 oz highball glass, with slice of orange and cherry for garnish.

# Pinchgut Peril

Created by Chevron Hotel

½ oz gin
1 oz whisky
½ oz lime juice
2 dashes Grenadine
½ slice pineapple

ice
shaved ice
pineapple pieces
slice orange

Mix gin, whisky, lime juice, Grenadine and pineapple with ice in electric mixer.
Pour onto shaved ice in a highball glass.
Decorate with pineapple and slice of orange and serve.


# Pink Angel

Created by John Grech

1 oz Bacardi
½ oz Advokaat
½ oz Cherry Brandy

egg white
1 oz fresh cream

Shake Bacardi, Advokaat, Cherry Brandy, egg white and cream.
Strain into champagne glass and serve.


# Pink Mintie

Created by James Smith

1 oz fresh cream
1 dash Grenadine

1 oz Crème de Menthe
ice

Shake cream, Grenadine and Crème de Menthe with ice.
Serve in 3 oz cocktail glass.


# Potts Point Special

Created by Chevron Hotel

⅓ unsweetened pineapple juice
⅓ Vodka
⅓ White Curaçao

ice
¼ slice pineapple

Shake pineapple, Vodka, Curaçao with ice.
Pour into champagne glass with ¼ slice of pineapple and serve.

# Purple Shell
Created by Peter Cowie

¾ Sloe Gin
½ oz gin

½ oz Parfait Amour
1½ oz fresh cream

Shake gin, Parfait Amour and cream.
Strain into 5 oz champagne glass and serve.


# Salubrious Salutations
Created by Peter Cowie

½ oz Galliano
½ oz Drambuie
½ oz gin

½ oz Benedictine
1 oz fresh cream

Shake Galliano, Drambuie, gin, Benedictine and cream.
Strain into 3 oz cocktail glass and serve.


# Snoopy's Gleam
Created by Noel Sylvester

1 oz Bourbon
¼ oz Orange Curaçao
¼ oz Grenadine

½ oz orangeade
slice orange
1 Maraschino cherry

Shake Bourbon, Curaçao, Grenadine and orangeade.
Serve in 2½ oz cocktail glass with garnish of orange and cherry.


# Sonja
Created by Tony Warby

1 oz Yellow Chartreuse
½ oz Blue Curaçao
½ oz Galliano

fresh cream
nutmeg
1 Maraschino cherry

Stir Chartreuse, Curaçao and Galliano.
Strain into 2½ oz cocktail glass and float cream on top.
Sprinkle with nutmeg, garnish with cherry and serve.

# Southerly Buster
Created by Frank Ferrucci

2 cubes ice
1 oz brandy
½ oz dry vermouth

½ oz lime cordial
dry ginger ale
slice lemon

In 10 oz highball glass add ice, brandy, vermouth and lime cordial.
Fill up with dry ginger ale.
Serve with drinking straws and slice of lemon.


# Southerly Kiss
Created by John Grech

1 sugar cube
¼ oz dry gin

1 oz Parfait Amour
champagne

Add gin to sugar cube.
Top up with champagne.
Pour Parfait Amour down side of champagne glass and serve.


# Sunset
Created by Michael Elliott

1 oz Cherry Brandy
1 oz Advokaat

1 oz fresh cream
lemonade

Pour Cherry Brandy, Advokaat and cream into 10 oz highball glass.
Top with lemonade and serve.


# Swiss Chocolate
Created by Tony Warby

fresh cream
⅓ Anisette
⅓ Green Tea

⅓ Cherry Brandy
1 Maraschino cherry

Float cream on top of Anisette, Green Tea and Cherry Brandy in 3 oz
cocktail glass.
Garnish with cherry and serve.

# Top of The Cross
Created by Michael Elliott

1 oz Pernod
1 oz Blue Curaçao

ginger beer

Top Pernod and Curaçao with ginger beer.
Serve in 10 oz highball glass.


# Travelex
Created by Hans Ubelhak

½ oz Galliano
¼ oz Vodka
¼ oz Marie Bizard Crème de Bananes

½ oz lemon juice
2 teaspoons Kummel
piece pineapple for decoration
ice

Shake all ingredients over ice.
Pour into 3 oz cocktail glass.
Decorate with pineapple and serve.


# Transplant
Created by David Bethune

1 oz Bacardi
1 small dash Galliano
1 small dash green Crème de Menthe

pure orange juice
spiral orange peel

Top Bacardi, Galliano and Crème de Menthe with orange juice.
Garnish with spiral orange peel and serve in 10 oz highball glass.

# True Blue

Created by John Grech

crushed ice
½ oz Crème de Cacao
½ oz Maraschino

½ oz Bacardi
fresh cream
1 Maraschino cherry

Add crushed ice to champagne glass.
Shake Crème de Cacao, Maraschino and Bacardi.
Strain into glass.
Top with fresh cream.
Garnish with cherry and serve.


# Wild Jaffa

Created by Tony Warby

⅓ Galliano
⅓ Vodka
⅓ Cointreau
dash lemon juice

dash Gomme Syrup (sugar syrup)
3 drops Grenadine

Shake all ingredients except Grenadine.
Strain into 3 oz cocktail glass with 3 drops Grenadine in the bottom and serve.


# Yerrep Cocktail

Created by Tony Camilleri

1 oz Advokaat
¼ oz Grand Marnier
1 tablespoon ice cream
1 oz fresh cream

2 dashes Ricard
1 Maraschino cherry for decoration

Shake all ingredients.
Strain into champagne glass.
Decorate with cherry on the side and serve.

# CHAMPAGNE COCKTAILS

Of all the sparkling wines champagne is one of the best. Infinite care goes into bringing the bottle of champagne to the remarkable degree of perfection which justifies its high price. The bubbles of sparkling champagne are the same as the bubbles of bottled beer: they are tiny drops of liquid, disturbed. whipped and chased by escaping carbonic acid gas at the time of fermentation. Champagne should always be served cold but not over-iced. It usually has a golden straw colour but there is also pink champagne.

'Feminine grace, feminine goodness, and feminine generosity; may they exist forever.'

# Black Velvet

½ champagne (chilled)                    ½ stout (chilled)

Pour champagne and stout simultaneously and slowly into champagne glass and serve.


# Champagne Cocktail

See photograph opposite page 64.

cube sugar                              chilled champagne
Angostura bitters                       twist lemon
½ oz brandy

In champagne glass put cube of sugar.
Saturate with bitters.
Add brandy.
Fill with chilled champagne.
Stir only to dissolve sugar.
Serve with twist of lemon.


# Mimosa Cocktail

½ orange juice (chilled)                 ½ champagne (chilled)

In champagne glass pour orange juice and champagne and serve.

# ASSORTED DRINKS

Collins; Coolers; Crustas; Daisies; Egg Noggs; Fixes; Fizzers; Flips; Frappes; Gimlet; Highball; Old-fashioned; Rickeys; Slings; Smashes; Sours; Toddies.

'My heart is as big as my glass when I drink to you good friend.'

# COLLINS

These are long drinks which should be served in a 10 oz highball glass and there are recipes by the dozen. Before 1939 a 'John Collins' was made with Dutch Gin and 'Tom Collins' with 'Old Tom' Gin. Nowadays Tom Collins is made with dry gin. John Collins is made with Dutch Gin.

## Tom Collins

cracked ice
2 oz lemon juice
1 teaspoon sugar
2 oz dry gin

soda water
slice lemon
1 Maraschino cherry

Put cracked ice, lemon juice, sugar and gin in glass.
Fill with soda water and stir.
Serve with slice of lemon and cherry for garnish.
NOTE:   Brandy, Bourbon, Rum or any whisky can be used instead of gin.

## COOLERS

These 'cousins' to the Collins drinks are also summer or hot weather drinks, as they are long and refreshing and made with plenty of ice.

## Rum Cooler

2 oz lemon juice
4 dashes Grenadine
2 oz rum

cracked ice
soda water
fruit for garnish

Shake lemon juice, Grenadine and rum well with ice.
Strain into 10 oz glass.
Add cracked ice.
Fill with soda water.
Garnish with any fruit and serve.
NOTE:   Wine or whisky can be used instead of rum.

# Gin Cooler

cracked ice
1/2 tablespoons sugar
2 oz lemon juice

2 oz gin
ginger beer
fruit for garnish

Put ice in glass. Add sugar, lemon juice and gin.
Fill with ginger beer.
Garnish with any fruit and serve.

# CRUSTAS

To be served in champagne glass.
Firstly rub rim of glass with slice of lemon and dip into plate containing
castor sugar.

# Brandy Crusta

1 dash Angostura bitters
3 oz brandy

3 dashes Maraschino
1 Maraschino cherry

Shake bitters, brandy and Maraschino.
Strain into champagne glass.
Add cherry and serve.
NOTE:   Gin, rum or whisky can be substituted for brandy. In some
parts of the world it is common to add 1 tsp lemon juice and 2 tsps
orange juice to this recipe.

# DAISIES

These are pleasant iced drinks lavishly decorated with fresh fruit and
refreshing for summer.
To be served in 6 oz goblet.

# Brandy Daisy

cracked ice
2 oz brandy
1 oz lemon juice

6 dashes Grenadine
soda water
fruit and mint for decoration

Fill goblet with cracked ice.
Shake brandy, lemon juice and Grenadine.
Strain and add soda water.
Decorate with fruit and sprigs of mint and serve.
NOTE:   Gin, rum or whisky can be substituted for brandy.

# EGG NOGGS

Egg noggs are delicious served warm or cold. They are very rich so if making for several people it is wiser to make small amounts for one or two glasses go a long way.

## Egg Nogg

1 egg
1 tablespoon sugar
1 oz brandy

milk
nutmeg

Shake egg, sugar and brandy well. Strain into 10 oz glass.
Fill with milk.
Sprinkle nutmeg on top and serve.
NOTE:   Gin, rum or whisky can be substituted for brandy.

# FIXES

To be served in 6 oz glass with shaved ice.

## Brandy Fix

1 oz brandy
1 oz Cherry Brandy
1 teaspoon sugar

1 teaspoon water
1 oz lemon juice
slice of lemon

Stir brandy, Cherry Brandy, sugar, water and lemon juice.
Add slice of lemon and serve.
NOTE:   Rum, gin and whisky fixes are made as above but minus brandy and Cherry Brandy.

# FIZZES

Another drink similar to those in the Collins family.
To be served in 7 oz glass.

# Bacardi Fizz

2 oz Bacardi Rum  
1 teaspoon sugar  
2 oz lemon juice

ice  
soda water

Shake rum, sugar and lemon juice well with ice and strain.  
Fill with soda water and serve.  
NOTE:   Gin, any whisky, or brandy can be used instead of rum.

Golden Fizz is spirit fizz plus yolk of egg.  
Silver Fizz is spirit fizz plus white of egg.

# FLIPS

The Flip, and particularly the variety made with rum is renowned as an old-fashioned drink. It once was very popular among sailors.  
To be served in 6 oz goblet.

# Brandy Flip

2 oz brandy  
1 teaspoon sugar  
1 whole egg

ice  
nutmeg

Shake brandy, sugar and egg with ice.  
Strain.  
Sprinkle nutmeg on top and serve.  
NOTE:   Rum, whisky, claret, port, sherry or blackberry brandy can be used instead of brandy.

# FRAPPES

Frappés can be made from any liquor or liqueur or combination of both.  
The simplest method is to fill a 5 oz glass with shaved ice and pour 1 oz of the liqueur you desire over it. Serve with drinking straw. See photograph opposite page 96.

# GIMLET

This drink has a very interesting history. It started its life on the sailing ships of old, travelling the Atlantic. Due to lack of vitamins in the diet of the sailors on board these ships, the crew very often suffered from scurvy. To counteract this, they were issued with fresh limes high in vitamin C which were able to be stored. To encourage the sailors to eat this fruit, they were issued with a tot of gin to mix with the juice of the lime and so the 'Gimlet' was born.

## Gimlet Cocktail

ice
⅔ dry gin

⅓ Roses lime juice
twist of lemon

In mixing glass put ice, add gin and lime juice.
Stir.
Strain into 3 oz cocktail glass.
Serve with twist of lemon (as limes not available here).

# HIGHBALL

The story of the 'Highball' goes back to the days when the railways were being constructed in the United States. As each section of the railway was completed, a signal was raised, usually a telegraph pole with a large white disc on it. When the men saw the 'Highball' raised they knew that it was time for a rest period which consisted of a long cool drink which was not strong, but stimulating and thirst quenching.

# Bourbon Highball

ice
2 dashes bitters
2 oz Bourbon

soda water or dry ginger ale
twist of lemon

Place ice in 10 oz glass.
Add bitters and Bourbon.
Fill with soda water or dry ginger ale.
Garnish with twist of lemon and serve.
NOTE: Brandy, gin, Irish, rum, rye, scotch, Tequila or Applejack may be used instead of Bourbon.


# Horse's Neck

lemon
4 cubes ice
1½ oz brandy

2 dashes Angostura bitters
dry ginger ale

Peel the skin of a lemon in one piece.
Place one end of the peel over the edge of a 10 oz highball glass (giving the effect of a horse's neck).
Fill glass with ice cubes.
Add brandy, Angostura bitters.
Top with dry ginger ale and serve.


# Old-Fashioned Cocktail
See photograph opposite page 32.

1 dash bitters
1 cube of sugar
2 dashes soda water or water
ice

2 oz Rye Whisky
½ slice orange
1 Maraschino cherry
twist of lemon

Use old-fashioned glass.
Put dash of bitters on cube of sugar
Add 2 dashes soda water or water.
Muddle this.
Add ice.
Add 2 oz Rye Whisky.
Place ½ slice of orange and cherry on toothpick on side of glass.
Put twist of lemon in glass and serve with swizzle stick.
NOTE: Most popular spirit used is Rye or Bourbon, but any base can be used.

Brandy Alexander, Blue Curacao Frappe, Manhattan (Rye Whisky)

TOP: l to r: Old Fashioned; double old fashioned; 10 oz Highball; 12 oz Highball or Zombie; Liqueur or cordial; Whisky; Shot

CENTRE: l to r: Wine (red); Wine (white); Sherry; Brandy Balloon or Snifter

BOTTOM: l to r: Martini glass; glass ice bucket; martini mixing glass; bar spoon

# Manhattan

See photograph opposite page 96.

⅔ Rye Whisky                    dash of Angostura bitters
⅓ sweet vermouth            1 Maraschino cherry

Stir whisky, vermouth and bitters in mixing glass.
Strain into cocktail glass.
Garnish with cherry and serve.
NOTE:   This can be made with Bourbon instead of Rye Whisky.


# RICKEYS

These long drinks keep to a spirit for their base, adding both juice and rind of a lime or lemon. The glass is filled with iced soda water or other charged water.
Serve in 6 oz glass.


# Gin Rickey

2 oz gin                        soda water
1 oz lime juice             lemon rind
ice

Pour gin and lime juice into glass over ice.
Top with soda water.
Serve with rind of lemon in glass.
NOTE:   Applejack, Bourbon, rum or any whisky can be substituted for gin.


# SLINGS

Properly made the contemporary Sling should be of brandy, whisky or gin base, with or without sugar and nutmeg, according to the other ingredients used and taste.
Use 10 oz highball glass filled with ice.

# Gin Sling

See photograph opposite page 48.

ice
2 oz gin
1 oz lemon juice
dash Grenadine

soda water or water
slice of lemon
1 Maraschino cherry

Pour gin, lemon juice and Grenadine into glass.
Top with soda water or water.
Garnish with slice of lemon and cherry and serve.
NOTE: Brandy, rum and whisky can be used instead of gin.

# Singapore Sling

2 oz gin
1 oz Cherry Brandy
1 oz lemon juice

soda water
slice lemon or orange
sprig of mint

Pour gin, Cherry Brandy and lemon juice into glass.
Top with soda water.
Garnish with slice of lemon or orange and sprig of mint and serve.
NOTE: 2 oz Sloe Gin can be substituted for 2 oz gin and 1 oz Cherry Brandy.

# SMASHES

Another member of the Collins family, the Smash is almost a cross between a Mint Julep and an Old-Fashioned without the fruit garnish. Serve in old-fashioned glass.

# Brandy Smash

1 teaspoon sugar
water
2 sprigs mint

cracked ice
2 oz brandy

Dissolve sugar with little water and sprigs of mint.
Muddle this and add cracked ice.
Pour brandy over ice.
Decorate with mint and serve with drinking straws.
NOTE: Gin, rum or any whisky can be used instead of brandy.

# SOURS

Serve in 6 oz glass.

## Whisky Sour

2 oz Canadian Whisky
1 oz lemon juice
½ teaspoon sugar
few drops egg white

soda water
slice orange
1 Maraschino cherry

Shake whisky, lemon juice, sugar and egg white and strain.
Top with soda water.
Garnish with slice orange and cherry and serve.
NOTE: Any whisky, Bourbon, or Tequila can be used.

# TODDIES

Serve in old-fashioned glass or mug.

## Brandy Toddy

1 teaspoon sugar
water

ice cubes
2 oz brandy

Dissolve sugar with little water in glass.
Add ice cubes and brandy.
Stir and serve.
NOTE: Bacardi, Calvados, gin or whisky can be substituted for brandy.

## Hot Toddies
Served in old-fashioned glass or mug.

1½ oz any spirit
1 teaspoon sugar
2 cloves

1 slice lemon
1 stick cinnamon

Mix spirit, sugar, cloves, lemon and cinnamon.
Add boiling water over silver spoon in glass (to prevent glass cracking).
Serve.

# MISCELLANEOUS COCKTAILS

'May we have more friends and need them less and less.'

# Americano Cocktail

3 cubes ice
1 oz Campari bitters
2 oz sweet vermouth

soda water
twist lemon peel

In a tall glass put ice cubes, bitters and vermouth.
Top with soda water.
Add twist of lemon peel.
Stir and serve.


# Angel's Kiss

There are many variations of this after dinner drink but we will leave
it up to you to choose your own 'Angel's Kiss'.

No. 1
¾ oz Apricot Liqueur
No. 2
¼ oz Crème de Cacao
¼ oz Crème de Violette

¼ oz thick cream floated on top

¼ Prunelle
¼ oz fresh cream

These ingredients are poured carefully into a pousse café glass in the
order given so the different liqueurs do not mix.
No. 3
1/6 Maraschino Liqueur
1/6 Parfait Amour
1/6 Yellow Chartreuse

1/6 Benedictine
1/6 Cognac
1/6 fresh cream

These ingredients are poured carefully into a pousse café glass in the
order given so the different liqueurs do not mix.


# Angel's Lips

⅔ oz Benedictine

⅓ oz fresh cream floated on top
in liqueur glass

# Bullshot

1 cube beef stock  
2 oz hot water  
¼ tablespoon celery salt or salt  
fresh lemon

1-1¼ oz Vodka  
ice  
lemon peel

Dissolve stock cube in hot water.  
Add celery salt or salt, squeeze of fresh lemon and Vodka.  
Stir vigorously.  
Serve on the rocks in old-fashioned glass with lemon peel garnish.  
NOTE: Rum can be substituted for Vodka in the above recipe.

# Cafe Royale

1 lump sugar  
demi-tasse cup hot black coffee

1 teaspoon brandy

Place sugar in a teaspoon and balance over a demi-tasse cup of hot coffee.  
Fill the spoon with brandy and when warm blaze with lighted match.  
As the flame begins to fade, put the spoon into the coffee, and then serve.

# Egg Sour

1 tablespoon castor sugar  
juice of ¼ lemon  
1 oz White Curaçao

1 oz brandy  
1 whole egg  
cracked ice

Shake castor sugar, lemon juice, Curaçao, brandy and egg with cracked ice.  
Strain into sour glass and serve.

# French 95 Made with Bourbon whiskey instead of gin.
See **FRENCH 75** under Gin Cocktails.

# French 125 Made with brandy instead of gin.
See **FRENCH 75** under Gin Cocktails.

# Grasshopper

See photograph opposite page 49.

1 oz white Crème de Cacao          2 oz fresh cream
1½ oz green Crème de Menthe       cracked ice

Shake Crème de Cacao, Crème de Menthe and cream with ice.
Strain into champagne glass and serve.


# Jack Rose

1½ oz Applejack                    juice of ½ lemon
1 tablespoon Grenadine

Shake Applejack, Grenadine and lemon juice.
Strain into cocktail glass and serve.


# Negroni

1 oz dry gin                       ice
½ oz Campari bitters               soda water
¾ oz sweet vermouth                lemon peel

Stir gin, bitters and vermouth in mixing glass with ice. Pour into 5 or
6 oz glass.
Add splash of soda water and lemon peel and serve.

# New Orleans Fizz

2 oz dry gin
1 oz lemon juice
1 rounded teaspoon sugar
1 oz sweet cream
white of 1 egg

2 or 3 dashes orange flower water
1 dash vanilla
cracked ice
soda water

Shake all ingredients with cracked ice until thoroughly mixed and frothy. Strain into 10 oz highball glass. Fill with soda water and serve.

# Pimm's
The original and best-known is Pimm's No 1 cup with gin base.

3 cubes ice
1½ oz Pimm's No 1
ginger ale (or lemonade)

slice cucumber
slice orange
1 Maraschino cherry

In 10 oz glass pour ice cubes.
Add 1½ oz Pimm's No 1.
Top with ginger ale (or lemonade if preferred).
Garnish with slice of cucumber, slice of orange and cherry, and serve.

# Pousse Cafe (original recipe)

1/6 oz Grenadine
1/6 oz Crème de Cacao dark liqueur
1/6 oz Maraschino liqueur

1/6 oz Green Crème de Menthe liqueur
1/6 oz Crème Yvette liqueur
1/6 oz brandy

Pour the liqueurs into a 1 oz liqueur glass over the back of a spoon, held so that it touches the edge of the inside of the glass. The pouring must be done very carefully to prevent the liqueurs mixing. Placing the liqueurs one on top of the other takes patience and make sure they are poured in the order given above.
The recipe as photographed consists of 1 part Grenadine, 1 part Maraschino and 1 part Blue Curaçao. See photograph opposite page 112.
NOTE: Pour the ingredients in the order given in the recipe as liqueurs differ in weight.

# Ramoz Fizz

2 oz dry gin
1 oz lemon juice
1 oz lime juice
1 oz heavy cream

2 dashes of orange flower water
1 egg white
1 teaspoon sugar
cracked ice

Shake above ingredients vigorously and thoroughly with cracked ice.
Strain into 8 or 10 oz highball glass with edge frosted with lemon and
sugar, and serve.


# Shandy

½ beer

½ lemonade


# Zazerac

1 cube sugar
1 dash Angostura bitters
1 dash soda water
3 ice cubes
1 oz Bourbon or Rye

½ teaspoon Pernod or Ricard
1 slice orange
1 Maraschino cherry
lemon peel

Put cube of sugar in old-fashioned glass.
Add Angostura bitters.
Dissolve sugar with bitters and soda water.
Add ice and Bourbon or Rye.
Float Pernod or Ricard on top.
Garnish with slice of orange on one side and cherry on the other side.
Put lemon peel in glass and serve with swizzle stick.

# PICK–ME–UPS

BOOZE!   BOOZE!   The breakfast of champions!
The 'morning after' misery is due to the effects of ethyl alcohol
in your blood — your tongue is parched and feels as if you have
licked the envelopes of all your Christmas mail in one night. You
are cursing yourself for having that 'last one for the road' for now
you have a first-rate hangover. But work must go on and you will
not get sympathy from your boss nor your wife. Wherever you
go you are told of sure-fire hangover cures but usually these are
vile-tasting concoctions and don't work completely. But at least
they give some consolation.

  Upon rising, try deep breathing for this will send oxygen to your
brain. And then try one of these simple remedies:

'Long life to you, and may you not be ill during the year for as long
as it takes you to swallow your drink.'

# 1  Fernet Branca

This is a thick black bitters with quinine

1½ oz Fernet Branca                    1½ oz Pernod

Mix in old-fashioned glass with ice.

# 2  Prairie Oyster

In a champagne glass sprinkle Worcestershire sauce
2 drops Tabasco
yolk of fresh egg
sprinkle salt and pepper
Down in one gulp.

# 3  Red Eye

½ cold beer                            ½ tomato juice

Mix beer with tomato juice.
Serve in 10 oz glass.

# 4  Pick-Me-Up No 1

⅓ Cognac                               ⅓ Pernod
⅓ dry vermouth

Stir ingredients and strain into 6 oz glass for serving.

# 5  Pick-Me-Up No 2

dash Angostura bitters                 milk
1 teaspoon sugar                       soda water
2 oz brandy

In 10 oz glass put bitters, sugar and brandy.
Fill glass with milk.
Shake and strain and add squirt of soda water.

# 6  Eddie's Cure

2 headache powders                     1 glass water

Return to bed with this book.

# PUNCHES

In its oldest and simplest form Punch was Rum and water, hot or cold, with sugar to taste and orange or lemon juice (for Hot Punch) or fresh lime juice (for Cold Punch). During the eighteenth century this drink was very popular and was 'brewed' at the table in a punchbowl by the host with Rum as one of the ingredients but with other spirits as well.

'Here's to the love that lies in woman's eyes — and lies and lies.'

# A.B.G. Punch

To make approximately 25 drinks

½ gallon vanilla ice cream
½ bottle (13 oz) sweet vermouth

1 bottle (26 oz) Bourbon
Maraschino cherries

Place ice cream in bowl and mix vermouth in slowly, then add Bourbon.
Add some cherries and serve.


# Brandy Alexander Punch

You will need for 12 persons

cracked ice
1 bottle (26 oz) brandy
½ bottle (13 oz) Crème de Cacao

3 pints fresh cream
nutmeg
Maraschino cherries

Place cracked ice in punch bowl.
Mix all ingredients with egg-beater till mixture starts to thicken.
Dust with nutmeg.
Add Maraschino cherries (optional) and serve.


# Judy's Punch

(Non-alcoholic)
To make approximately 20 drinks

Use any fruit in season or 2 tins
fruit salad in punch bowl
Add cracked ice
13 oz lemon cordial

8 dashes Angostura bitters
1 - 32 oz bottle lemonade
1 - 32 oz bottle soda water
2 oz Grenadine for colouring

Mix all ingredients and serve with fruit from bowl.

# Kissing The Bride Punch
You will need for 12 persons

1 punnet strawberries
icing sugar

6 oz Cognac
2 bottles champagne

Place strawberries in punch bowl and cover with icing sugar.
Add Cognac and refrigerate for 6 to 8 hours.
Before serving, add champagne (well iced).
NOTE:   It is not necessary to add ice to this punch.


# Party Punch
To make approximately 25 drinks

1 bottle Southern Comfort
(26 oz)
4 oz Jamaican Rum
4 oz lemon juice
8 oz pineapple juice

8 oz grapefruit juice
2 bottles champagne
(26 oz each)
cracked or chipped ice
orange slices for garnish

Cool all ingredients then mix in punch bowl.
Add champagne last and ice either cracked or chipped.
Garnish with orange slices and serve.


# Teetotaller's Punch
(Non-alcoholic)
To make approximately 20 drinks

½ bottle (13 oz) Clayton's Tonic
3 oz lemon juice
10 dashes of Angostura bitters

2 – 26 oz bottles dry ginger ale
1 – 26 oz bottle lemonade
lemon slices

Mix all ingredients with cracked ice in punch bowl and lemon slices
and serve.

# Tom and Jerry
(Hot Punch)

eggs
1 teaspoon castor sugar
1 oz brandy
1 oz Jamaican Rum

hot water
hot milk
nutmeg

Take as many eggs as persons to be served.
Beat the whites and yolks separately.
Add 1 teaspoon of castor sugar for each egg and mix whites with yolks.
When ready to serve, take 2 tablespoons of the egg mixture and put in a large mug.
Add 1 oz brandy and 1 oz Jamaican Rum (mixed together to avoid curdling).
Fill to the top with hot water or hot milk or half of each and stir until smooth.
Sprinkle nutmeg on top and serve.
NOTE:   This recipe can be made with Bourbon and brandy also.

# NON–
# ALCOHOLIC
# COCKTAILS

'Here's to woman – once our superior, now our equal.'

Pousse Café

Cocktail cabinet (Whisky Sour – Rye Whisky) in foreground

# Boo Boo's Special

ice
¼ oz lemon juice
3 oz pineapple juice
3 oz orange juice

1 dash Angostura bitters
1 dash Grenadine
water
pineapple or fruit in season

In cocktail shaker with ice mix lemon juice, pineapple juice, orange juice, Angostura bitters and Grenadine.
Shake and serve in tall highball glass.
Top with water.
Garnish with pineapple or fruit in season.

# Egg Nogg

1 egg
1 teaspoon castor sugar
10 oz milk

ice
nutmeg or cinnamon
1 Maraschino cherry

Shake egg, castor sugar and milk with ice.
Strain into tall highball glass and dust with nutmeg or cinnamon.
Garnish with cherry and serve with drinking straw.

# Lemonade

cracked ice
juice of 1 lemon
2 tablespoons sugar

water
1 slice lemon

Fill tall glass with cracked ice.
Add lemon juice and sugar.
Shake and pour unstrained into glass.
Top with water.
Slice lemon in drink.
Serve with drinking straws.

# Mickey Mouse

ice
coca cola
1 scoop ice cream

whipped cream
2 Maraschino cherries

In tall glass with ice pour coca cola.
Add 1 scoop ice cream.
Top with whipped cream.
Serve with 2 cherries, drinking straw and spoon.

# GLOSSARY

**ADVOKAAT** — A Dutch liqueur made from egg yolks, sugar and brandy.

**AERATED WATER** — Mineral water.

**ALMOND SYRUP** — Syrup made of sweet almonds and water.

**AMER PICON** — A French aperitif wine.

**AMOURETTE** — A violet-coloured French liqueur.

**AMSTERDAM** — A liqueur containing Cherry Brandy and Advokaat.

**ANGELICA** — A very sweet Basque liqueur flavoured with angelica.

**ANISETTE** — A very sweet colourless aniseed-flavoured liqueur.

**APERITIF** — Low alcoholic content drink taken before meals and designed to sharpen the appetite.

**APPLE BRANDY OR APPLEJACK** — Brandy distilled from apple wine.

**APPLE CIDER** — Fermented apple juice.

**APRICOT BRANDY** — A highly-flavoured liqueur made from apricots.

**AQUAVIT** — Scandinavian liqueur made from potatoes and flavoured with caraway seeds.

**ARMAGNAC** — A French grape brandy.

**ARRACK** — Any Eastern spirituous liquor, especially one made from coco palm. Different countries use various ingredients but rice is also commonly used in this liquor.

**AURUM** — A pale gold Italian liqueur of orange flavour — not too sweet.

**BENEDICTINE D.O.M.** — A sweet, herb-flavoured, brandy-based liqueur. One of the oldest liqueurs in the world and originally made by Benedictine monks. Can be mixed with equal parts of brandy and known as B. & B. Benedictine is sometimes referred to as D.O.M. liqueur (*Deo optimo maximo*) of the Benedictine Order.

**BITTERS** — An infusion of aromatics. Contains roots and herbs and is used sparingly to flavour cocktails. Can also be used as a pick-me-up. Best-known brands are Angostura, Fernet Branca and Peychauds.

**BLACKBERRY BRANDY** — A very dark liqueur flavoured with blackberries.

**BLACKCURRANT LIQUEUR** — Liqueur made from blackcurrants, brandy and sugar; also known under its French name Cassis.

**BOILERMAKER** — A shot of straight Scotch followed by beer chaser.

**BOOMERANGO** — An Australian liqueur with banana and cinnamon flavour.

**BRANDY** — Distilled from fermented juices of ripe grapes and other fruits. When sweetening is added it then is usually referred to as a liqueur.

**BRONTE** — A brandy based liqueur with honey taste.

**BYRRH** — A French aperitif.

**CALVADOS** — Apple brandy from Normandy.

| | |
|---|---|
| **CAMPARI** | An Italian aperitif wine with strong bitter taste. |
| **CHAMBERY** | A very dry vermouth from the district of Chambery, France. |
| **CHARTREUSE** | A liqueur made from many different roots, spices and herbs. There are two types: yellow which is light, and green which is heavy and stronger in spirit strength. |
| **CHERI-SUISE** | A chocolate cherry liqueur. |
| **CHERRY BRANDY** | A liqueur containing juice of ripe cherries. |
| **CHIANTI** | Dry Italian wine mostly red in colour but white is available. |
| **CLAYTON'S TONIC** | Non-alcoholic kola. |
| **CLEOPATRA** | A brown liqueur with chocolate and orange flavour. |
| **COINTREAU** | A sweet, colourless liqueur with orange flavour. |
| **CORDIAL-MEDOC** | A dark red French liqueur. |
| **CREME DE BANANE** | A brandy-based liqueur with banana flavour. |
| **CREME DE CASSIS** | A liqueur with blackcurrant flavour. |
| **CREME DE CACAO** | A very sweet dark brown liqueur made from cocoa beans, vanilla and spices and has cocoa flavour. |
| **CREME DE FRAISES** | A sweet French liqueur, strawberry in colour and flavoured with strawberries. |
| **CREME DE FRAMBOISES** | A sweet French liqueur, raspberry in colour and flavoured with raspberries. |
| **CREME DE MENTHE** | A peppermint-flavoured liqueur which comes in three colours — green, white or red. |
| **CREME DE MOKA** | A light brown French liqueur with coffee flavour. |
| **CREME DE NOYEAUX** | Almond flavoured French liqueur made from apricot and peach pits. Comes in pink and white. |
| **CREME DE ROSES** | A pink liqueur, flavoured with roses. |
| **CREME DE VANILLE** | A sweet French liqueur with strong vanilla flavour. |
| **CREME DE VIOLETTES** | A pale violet French liqueur with violet scent. |
| **CREME YVETTE** | A sweet American liqueur with the flavour, colour and scent of Parma violets. |
| **CURAÇAO** | A sweet digestive liqueur made with wine or grape spirit, sugar and peel from oranges grown on island of Curaçao — orange, blue, green and white colours. |
| **DAMSON GIN** | An English liqueur flavoured with damson and dark red in colour. |
| **DANZIGER** | A liqueur with gold leaf floating through it. |
| **DRAMBUIE** | A liqueur based on Scotch Whisky and heather honey. |
| **DUBONNET** | A dark red French aperitif wine with red wine base and a slight quinine taste. |
| **ELIXIR D'ANVERS** | A sweet yellow liqueur, similar taste to Yellow Chartreuse. |
| **FERNET BRANCA** | Italian bitters. |
| **FIOR D'ALPE** | A liqueur flavoured with flowers and herbs grown on slopes of the Alps. Extremely sweet — sugar forms crystals in bottle. |

| | |
|---|---|
| **FORBIDDEN FRUIT** | A red flame-coloured American liqueur. The flavour is mixture of grapefruit and orange, it is sweet with a bitter after-taste. |
| **FRAISIA** | A French liqueur red in colour with strawberry flavour. |
| **GALLIANO** | A gold-coloured liqueur with licorice and anisette flavour. |
| **GLAYVA** | A liqueur from Scotland, similar to Drambuie. |
| **GLEN MIST** | A liqueur similar to Drambuie, but containing mixture of Irish and Scottish whiskies. |
| **GOMME SYRUP** | Sugar syrup — made by heating 1 lb sugar in a pint of water, slowly stirring until it comes to the boil (do not let it boil). |
| **GRAND MARNIER** | A golden-brown French brandy liqueur, with orange flavour. |
| **GRAPPA** | Italian spirit made from the skins, pips and stalks of grapes after wine is made. |
| **GRANDE LIQUEUR** | A French liqueur made in two colours, yellow and green, with chartreuse flavour. |
| **GRENADINE** | Red artificial flavouring used for sweetness. |
| **GREEN GINGER WINE** | Wine made from fruit and Jamaican ginger. |
| **GOLDWASSER** | A colourless sweet liqueur with gold flakes, flavoured with orange and aniseed. |
| **IZZARA** | A yellow and green Basque country liqueur. |
| **KAHLUA** | A Mexican coffee liqueur made from coffee beans, cocoa beans, vanilla and brandy. |
| **KEUCK** | Dark-brown Turkish mocca liqueur. |
| **KIRSCH** | A colourless fruit brandy distilled from black cherries. |
| **KUMMEL** | A colourless liqueur flavoured with caraway seeds and cummin. |
| **LILLET** | A French aperitif with white wine base. |
| **LIQUEUR D'OR** | A golden sweet French liqueur with gold flakes. |
| **LIQUEUR JAUNE** | A yellow French liqueur similar to Yellow Chartreuse. |
| **LIQUEUR VERTE** | A French liqueur similar to Green Chartreuse. |
| **MARASCHINO** | A colourless cherry-flavoured liqueur originating in Italy. |
| **MARNIQUE** | An Australian liqueur similar to Grand Marnier. |
| **MARSALA** | A dark sherry-type wine from Sicily. |
| **MERRY WIDOW** | A gin base liqueur with coffee flavour. |
| **MONASTIQUE** | A South American liqueur similar to Benedictine. |
| **ORANGE BITTERS** | A bitter-sweet orange tasting flavouring. |
| **ORANGE FLOWER WATER** | From the Middle East with a delicate flavouring of orange blossom. |
| **OUZO** | A Greek liqueur with aniseed flavour. |
| **PARFAIT AMOUR** | A highly-scented French liqueur, light purple, in colour, and made from lemons, oranges, brandy and herbs. |
| **PEACH BRANDY** | A brandy-coloured liqueur, with peach flavour. |

| | |
|---|---|
| **PERNOD** | A French aperitif and ingredient for cocktails which is an imitation of Absinthe which was banned in France. Pernod 45 has aniseed flavour. Pernod Pastis has licorice flavour. |
| **PERRIER** | French mineral water. |
| **PEYCHAUDS** | **See** Bitters. |
| **PIMMS** | No 1 is most popular liquor with gin base. No 2 has whisky base. No 3 has brandy base. No 4 has rum base. No 5 has Rye Whiskey. No 6 has Vodka base. |
| **PISCO** | A clear white spirit from Peru with brandy flavour. |
| **PRUNELLE** | A pale-green liqueur with plum flavour. |
| **RICARD** | A yellow liqueur with aniseed flavour. |
| **RUMONA** | A liqueur with Jamaican rum base. |
| **ROSES LIME JUICE** | The most popular lime juice as used in gimlets. |
| **ROYAL CHOCOLATE LIQUEUR** | An opaque liqueur, with chocolate mint flavour. |
| **SABRA** | Liqueur from Israel, with chocolate and orange flavour. |
| **SAMBUCA** | An Italian liqueur with soft anisette flavour. |
| **SCHNAPPS** | **See** Aquavit. |
| **SEVEN-UP** | American soft drink similar to lemonade. |
| **SILVOVITZ** | European (Hungarian) liqueur flavoured with plums. |
| **SOUTHERN COMFORT** | An American liqueur with a brandy and Bourbon base and peach flavour. |
| **STREGA** | A light-coloured Italian liqueur, not sweet. |
| **SWEDISH PUNCH** | A highly alcoholic compound with a basis of rum or Arrack, flavoured with spices and other flavouring agents. |
| **TIA MARIA** | A Jamaican liqueur, based on rum, with coffee flavour. |
| **TRIPLE SEC** | White Curaçao. A colourless liqueur with sweet orange flavour. |
| **UNDERBERG** | German bitters. |
| **VAN DER HUM** | A South African liqueur with tangerine flavour. |
| **VIELLE CURE** | A brown French liqueur flavoured with herbs. |

# INDEX